Pronunciation and the Chaṇḍi Samputs

Swami Satyananda Saraswati
Shree Maa

Devi Mandir

Pronunciation and the Chaṇḍi Sampuṭs First edition

ISBN 978-1-877795-10-7
Library of Congress Catalog

Chaṇḍī Pāṭh, Swami Satyananda Saraswati
1. Hindu Religion. 2. Goddess Worship. 3. Spirituality.
4. Philosophy. I. Saraswati, Swami Satyananda.

Published by
Devi Mandir Publications
5950 Highway 128
Napa, CA 94558 USA
707-966-2802
www.shreemaa.org

Pronunciation and the Chaṇḍi Samputs

Every language has its own efficiencies, particularly expressive of the nature of those who communicate in that culture. "I make love in French, sing in Italian, give orders in German, and do business in English," was a favorite saying of an old friend. Saṁskṛt is a language descriptive of subtle states of consciousness. It is particularly efficient as a mode of prayer. It has a language which allows wisdom and devotion to unite in meditative states, capable of being expressed through every action we perform. Very few cultures have ever had occasion to think such thoughts, or the opportunity to experience such a quality of life, and as a consequence, they have never developed a vocabulary by which to express it. Saṁskṛt has.

The function of any language is to communicate. Saṁskṛt is an efficient medium by which to communicate with the Gods. The language has more words for expressing devotion than any other language. Just as Eskimos have more words for "Snow," Saṁskṛt is replete with a vocabulary for devotion and names of God. From the outset, Saṁskṛt Philosophy proclaims, "There is One God who has many names," and then the literature proceeds to fill many volumes with many names.

There is only one criteria for "Correct" Saṁskṛt pronunciation and understanding. Ramakrishna called it *Vyākulata*, an inner longing, a need or desire which is felt so intensely that we can think of nothing else, being entirely filled with it, expressed with a degree of sincerity that makes us pay attention to the exclusion of all other thoughts. That is what distinguishes "Correct" pronunciation in Saṁskṛt. Anything else can be the subject of endless debates, of regional cheauvanism, even Bollywood movies, but not the real purpose of Saṁskṛt.

This debate has been raging throughout history. There are even some who, like the French, may take the position that, "If you cannot pronounce correctly, it is better not to pronounce at all." And there are other statements to the effect that, "It is possible to receive injury or put yourself at a disadvantaged position, if you pronounce incorrectly or say the wrong thing."

We consider such statements as absurd and useless, tantamount to saying, "Unless I direct your prayer, it is of no value at all, or it is not a real prayer unless I lead it." It is absolutely ridiculous to think that God would not appreciate the sincerity of our efforts, even though we may make technical errors. The only examples in scriptures of people who have received adverse effects while praying, were for people who were praying for selfish desires. No where is there any reference to injury for individuals striving for self-purification, wisdom, or enlightenment, and certainly not for students who are trying to learn how to pronounce correctly in the first place.

Our goal is not to train puṁḍits. We are trying to inspire devotees around the world to pray with sincerity for blessings of good health, purity, and peace, inside themselves and around the world, in any language, in any tradition, any where, alone or with their families, in their own temples, in every temple, and to actualize that prayer in their every effort. We are not searching for Saṁskṛt experts. We are searching for real human beings. Our criteria is sincere longing to be with the Divine.

Therefore, this writing is an attempt to define why are there so many differences over pronunciation and what has given rise to this debate? What constitutes "Correct" pronunciation, and from where have the different versions of scriptures have arisen?

Throughout Saṁskṛt literature there are numerous examples of women who have attained to the heights of Godliness. Arundati, Lopāmudrā, Anasuyā, Sītā, Śabari, all are women who have proved that gender and caste are not criteria for spiritual attainment. The story of Satyakāma again shows that birth has no bearing on spiritual authority. Exactly who is authorized to recite which scriptures?

We will also explore some of the options for spiritual discipline using the recitation of the Chaṇḍi Pāṭh as our model.

Pronunciation and the Chaṇḍi Samputs

The Story of Vālmīkī

Vālmīkī was the most notorious robber of India. He used to ambush travellers all along the routes of Northern India, and steal their every valuable possession. Anyone who would offer even the slightest resistance would be killed. The reputation of Vālmīkī spread far and wide.

One day a sannyāsi was travelling along the road. Vālmīkī confronted him and demanded from him all his valuables. The sādhu replied, "I promise that I will give you everything, if you just answer one question for me."

"Ask your question," replied the thief.

"Will those with whom you share the wealth that you steal, also share your sins? You go ask them. I promise to wait right here until you bring me the answer."

Vālmīkī went home to his wife and said, "Wife, do you know what I do for a living?"

"Oh no, my husband. I only know that your duty is to bring home the food, and my duty is to prepare it and serve you and our family," came her reply.

"Well, my wife, I am a thief, a notorious bandit. I rob and steal and even kill people in order to feed our family. Will you share the sins that I accumulate, as well as the wealth that I bring home?"

"Oh no, my husband. I have no desire to share your sins. You fulfill your duty in the way you choose, and I will fulfill my own. But I won't take part in your sins!"

Vālmīkī went to his aged parents and asked, "Parents, do you know what I do for a living?"

The parents replied, "Oh no, Son. We only know that your duty is to bring home the food, and to take care of us, as we took care of you, when you were incapable of taking care of yourself," came their reply.

"Well, my parents, I am a thief, a notorious bandit. I rob and steal and even kill people in order to feed our family. Will you share the sins that I accumulate, as well as the wealth that I bring home?"

"Oh no, Son. We have no desire to share your sins. You fulfill your duty in the way you choose, as we fulfilled our own. But we won't take part in your sins!"

Vālmīkī went to his children and asked, "Children, do you know what I do for a living?"

The children replied, "Oh no, Father. We only know that your duty is to bring home the food, and to take care of us, as we will take care of you, when you will become incapable of taking care of yourself," came their reply.

"Well, my children, I am a thief, a notorious bandit. I rob and steal and even kill people in order to feed our family. Will you share the sins that I accumulate, as well as the wealth that I bring home?"

"Oh no, Father. We have no desire to share your sins. You fulfill your duty in the way you choose, as we will fulfill our own. But we won't take part in your sins!"

Vālmīkī returned to the sādhu who was waiting in the forest, and with great dejection he said, "Nobody is willing to share my sins. What shall I do to be free from all of the sins that I have accumulated?"

The sādhu proclaimed, "There is only one way to become free from sin. You must say the name of Rāma!"

"The name of Rāma!" cried Vālmīkī. "That name is so holy, I can't say that!"

The sannyāsi replied, "Well, then say Mārā, which means dead body. Certainly you can say that!"

Vālmīkī sat down and began to repeat Mārā, Mārā, Mārā, until the syllables joined together and became Rāma, Rāma, Rāma. He became so engrossed in the name, that he didn't even notice as the ants, Vālmīk, piled dirt over his body. Still he continued to recite the name of Rāma. When he awoke from his samādhi, he became know as Vālmīkī, He who came from the Ant Hill.

Vālmīkī was the author of the Rāmāyaṇa, and history attests to the conversion of the highwayman into a saint. Even though his pronunciation was not "Correct," because of his sincerity and absorption, Vālmīkī reached to greater spiritual attainment than the sannyāsi who gave him initiation.

Pronunciation and the Chaṇḍi Samputs

The debate over "Correct" pronunciation of Saṁskṛt is as old as the Vedas. Even the brāhmaṇa Deva Datta, who was performing the Putreṣṭhi Yajña, the special fire sacrifice to engender dharmic children, complained to Gobhila, the head priest officiating over the rites, about his pronunciation. "You're chanting like a fool without understanding!" he proclaimed.

Gobhila replied,

सर्वप्राणिशरीरे तु श्वासोच्छ्वासः सुदुर्ग्रहः ।

न मेऽत्र दूषणं किंचित्स्वरभंगे महामते ॥

sarvapÑāṇiśarīre tu śvāsocchvāsaḥ sudurgrahaḥ |
na me-tra dūṣaṇaṁ kiṁcitsvarabhaṁge mahāmate ||

सर्वप्राणिशरीरे **sarvapÑāṇiśarīre**

in the bodies of all that breathe

तु **tu** they have

श्वासोच्छ्वासः **śvāsocchvāsaḥ** inhalation and exhalation

सुदुर्ग्रहः **sudurgrahaḥ** difficult to control

न **na** not

मेऽत्र **me-tra** in me there

दूषणं **dūṣaṇaṁ** evil intent

किंचित **kiṁcit** any

स्वरभंगे **svarabhaṁge** to break the tune, melody

महामते **mahāmate** respected sir

Inhalation and exhalation existing in the bodies of all that breathe are difficult to control. Respected Sir, there is not any evil intention in me to break the tune or melody. Devi Bhagavatam 3:10:27

There are a number of issues that were raised by Gobhila's reply. The first is that he was using a system of Prāṇāyāma in his recitation, and that it was very difficult to perform or control. The second is that he had no evil intention, no selfish motivation, and therefore, his pronunciation was either pure or irrelevant.

It was the purity of his devotion that was important, his intention, and his effort. When Deva Datta again complained calling him a fool, Gobhila cursed him that his son would be born a fool! Deva Datta became extremely apologetic and fell prostrate at Gobhila's feet, begging for forgiveness. The muni relented and gave the boon that the ignorant son would ultimately become extremely wise, and would attain fame for his devotion to truth.

- 40 -

ईश्वरी सर्वभूतानां सर्वकारणकारणम् ।

सर्वकामार्थदा शांता सुखसेव्या दयान्विता ॥

īśvarī sarvabhūtānāṁ sarvakāraṇakāraṇam
sarvakāmārthadā śāṁtā sukhasevyā dayānvitā

ईश्वरी **īśvarī**

the Supreme Goddess

सर्वभूतानां **sarvabhūtānāṁ**

of all existence

सर्वकारणकारणम् **sarvakāraṇakāraṇam**

cause of all causes

सर्वकामार्थदा **sarvakāmārthadā**

giver of the objects of all desire

शांता **śāṁtā**

peace

सुखसेव्या **sukhasevyā**

who is served with happiness

दयान्विता **dayānvitā**

ocean of compassion

The Supreme Goddess of all existence, cause of all causes, giver of the objects of all desire, peace, who is served with happiness, the ocean of compassion,

- 41 -

नामोच्चारणमात्रेण वांछितार्थफलप्रदा ।

देवैराराधिता पूर्वं ब्रह्मविष्णुमहेश्वरैः ॥

nāmoccāraṇamātreṇa vāṁchitārthaphalapradā
devairārādhitā pūrvaṁ brahmaviṣṇumaheśvāraiḥ

नामोच्चारणमात्रेण **nāmoccāraṇamātreṇa**

merely pronouncing Her name

वांछितार्थफलप्रदा **vāṁchitārthaphalapradā**

bestows the fruit of objects of desire

देवैराराधिता **devairārādhitā**

who was propitiated by the Gods

पूर्वं **pūrvaṁ**

in days of old

ब्रह्मविष्णुमहेश्वरैः **brahmaviṣṇumaheśvāraiḥ**

and by Brahma, Viṣṇu, and Śiva

merely pronouncing Her name bestows the fruit of the objects of all desire. She who was propitiated by Brahmā, Viṣṇu, and Śiva, and by the Gods in days of old,

- 42 -

मोक्षकामैश्च विविधैस्तपसैर्विजितात्मभिः ।

अस्पष्टमपि यन्नाम प्रसंगेनापि भाषितम् ॥

mokṣakāmaiśca vividhaistapasairvijitātmabhiḥ
aspaṣṭamapi yannāma pÑsaṁgenāpi bhāṣitam

मोक्षकामैश्च **mokṣakāmaiśca**

and by those desiring liberation

विविधैस्तपसैर्विजितात्मभिः **vividhaistapasairvijitātmabhiḥ**

those who have mastered their own souls by means of various austerities

अस्पष्टमपि **aspaṣṭamapi**

even incorrectly, unintelligably, indiscernably

यन्नाम **yannāma**

Her name

प्रसंगेनापि **pÑsaṁgenāpi**

in praise

भाषितम् **bhāṣitam**

whoever speaks, proclaims

and by those desiring liberation, and those who have mastered their own souls by means of various austerities. To whomever proclaims Her name in praise even incorrectly,

- 43 -

ददाति वांछितानार्थान्दुर्लभानपि सर्वथा ।

ऐ ऐ इति भयार्तेन दृष्ट्वा व्याघ्रादिकं वने ॥

dadāti vāṁchitānārthāndurlabhānapi sarvathā
ai ai iti bhayārtena dṛṣṭvā vyāghrādikaṁ vane

दद‍ाति **dadāti**

She grants

वांछितानार्थान् **vāṁchitānārthān**

the desired objective

दुर्लभानपि **durlabhānapi**

even if it be difficult of attainment

सर्वथा **sarvathā**

always

ऐ ऐ इति **ai ai iti**

thus to one (who exclaimed) ai ai

भयार्तेन **bhayārtena**

because of fear

दृष्ट्वा **dṛṣṭvā**

upon seeing

व्याघ्रादिकं **vyāghrādikaṁ**

a tiger or other ferocious animals

वने **vane**

in the forest

She always grants the desired objective even though it be difficult of attainment. Thus to one who exclaimed "Ai, ai" upon seeing a tiger or other ferocious animals in the forest,

- 44 -

बिंदुहीनमपीत्युक्तं वांछितं प्रददाति वै ।

तत्र सत्यव्रतस्यैव दृष्टान्तो नृपसत्तम ॥

biṁduhīnamapītyuktaṁ vāṁchitaṁ pradadāti vai
tatra satyavratasyaiva dṛṣṭānto nṛpasattama

विंदुहीनमपीत्युक्तं **viṁduhīnamapītyuktaṁ**

even without being united with the bindu

वांछितं **vāṁchitaṁ**

the desire

प्रददाति **pÑdadāti**

She gave

वै **vai**

anyway, regardless

तत्र **tatra**

there

सत्यव्रतस्यैव **satyavÑtasyaiva**

SatyavÑta also

दृष्टान्तो **dṛṣṭānto**

can be seen

नृपसत्तम **nṛpasattama**

a most truthful King

even without being united with the bindu, She gave the desire anyway. There can also be seen (the story of) SatyavÑta, a most truthful King.

- 45 -

प्रत्यक्ष एव चास्माकं मुनीनां भावितात्मनाम् ।

ब्राह्मणानां समाजेषु तस्योदाहरणं बुधैः ॥

pÑtyakṣa eva cāsmākaṁ munīnāṁ bhāvitātmanām
bÑhmaṇānāṁ samājeṣu tasyodāharaṇaṁ budhaiḥ

प्रत्यक्ष **pÑtyakṣa**

has been perceived through the senses

एव **eva**

and

चास्माकं **cāsmākaṁ**

by us

मुनीनां **munīnāṁ**

wise people

भावितात्मनाम् **bhāvitātmanām**

very deep souls

ब्राह्मणानां समाजेषु **brāhmaṇānāṁ samājeṣu**

in the assemblies, congregations of brāhmaṇas, learned

तस्योदाहरणं **tasyodāharaṇaṁ**

there are many other examples

बुधैः **budhaiḥ**

are known

This has been perceived through the senses by us and by wise people and very deep souls, and there are many other examples known in the assemblies of the learned.

- 46 -

कथ्यमानं मया राजञ्छ्रुतं सर्वं सविस्तरम् ।

अनक्षरो महामूर्खो नाम्ना सत्यव्रतो द्विजः ॥

kathyamānaṁ mayā rājañchrutaṁ sarvaṁ savistaram
anakṣaro mahāmūrkho nāmnā satyavrato dvijaḥ

कथ्यमानं **kathyamānaṁ**

of the story

मया **mayā**

by me

राजञ् **rājañ**

oh king

छ्रुतं **chrutaṁ**

listen

सर्वं **sarvaṁ**

all, complete

सविस्तरम् **savistaram**

details

अनक्षरो **anakṣaro**

without letters, unlearned, illiterate, ignorant

महामूर्खो **mahāmūrkho**

a great fool

नाम्ना **nāmnā**

name

सत्यव्रतो **satyavrato**

Satyavrata

द्विजः **dvijaḥ**

a brāhmaṇa

Oh King, listen to the details of the story told by me, a brāhmaṇa. There was a great fool, completely ignorant, and his name was Satyavrata.

- 47 -

श्रुत्वाऽक्षरं कोलमुखात्समुच्चार्य स्वयं ततः ।
बिन्दुहीनं प्रसंगेन जातोऽसौ विबुधोत्तमः ॥

śrutvā-kṣaraṁ kolamukhātsamuccārya svayaṁ tataḥ
binduhīnaṁ pÑsaṁgena jāto-sau vibudhottamaḥ

श्रुत्वाऽक्षरं **śrutvā-kṣaraṁ**

hearing the letters, sounds

कोलमुखात् **kolamukhāt**

from the mouth of a pig

समुच्चार्य **samuccārya**

he began to pronounce

स्वयं **svayaṁ**

himself

ततः **tataḥ**

then

बिन्दुहीनं **binduhīnaṁ**

without the bindu (anusvara)

प्रसंगेन **prasaṁgena**

the consequence followed

जातोऽसौ **jāto-sau**

he became

विबुधोत्तमः **vibudhottamaḥ**

of excellent intelligence

Hearing the sounds from the mouth of a pig, he then began to pronounce them himself. Without the bindu (anusvara) (even still) the consequence followed that he became a man of excellent intelligence.

- 48 -

ऐकारोच्चारणाद्देवी तुष्टा भगवती तदा ।

चकार कविराजं तं दयार्द्रा परमेश्वरी ॥

aikāroccāraṇāddevī tuṣṭā bhagavatī tadā
cakāra kavirājaṁ taṁ dayārdrā parameśvārī

ऐकारोच्चारणाद्देवी **aikāroccāraṇāddevī**

From the pronunciation of the syllable ai the Goddess

तुष्टा **tuṣṭā**

satisfied

भगवती **bhagavatī**

Supreme Divinity

तदा **tadā**

then

चकार **cakāra**

made shine

कविराजं **kavirājaṁ**

king of poets

तं **taṁ**

him

दयार्द्रा **dayārdrā**

ocean of compassion

परमेश्वरी **parameśvārī**

Supreme Goddess

From the pronunciation of the syllable "Ai," the Goddess, the Supreme Divinity, became satisfied. Then the Supreme Goddess, the ocean of compassion, made him to shine as the king of poets.

Devi Bhagavatam 3:9:40-48

Deva Datta asked Gobhila to tell the story of Satyavrat.

The Story of Satyavrat

There was once a King named Aruna, born in the lineage of the decendants of Ikṣvāku. Aruna means love. Aruna's love is different from the love of passion and attachment. It is the love which makes men divine. Aruna was such a wonderful King and had so much Love, that ultimately he became the charioteer of Sūrya, the Sun. His kind of Love can be the driver of the conveyance of the Light Wisdom, so his is the universal love based in wisdom.

Aruna came to the earth several generations after Ikṣvāku had lived, and was born in the house of the Solar Dynasty. Aruna was a very righteous King. He treated his subjects like his own family, and always made decisions on the basis of equity, fairness, and justice. He was a valiant and noble King, who constantly acted with compassion and universal love and was never selfish.

He had a son by the name of Satyavrat, One who is True to his Vow. Satyavrat grew up in the palace, but even though his name was the One who is True to his Vow, he was always in trouble. He would run around with his friends and create havoc. Wherever he went, he would create another problem. In this way the child grew up always being scolded, but he never told a lie.

One day when Satyavrat was just a teenager, he came by a village of brāhmaṇas as they were conducting a marriage ceremony. Satyavrat rode in his own chariot, picked up the bride, put her in the chariot, and rode off with her.

The brāhmaṇas cried aghast, "Oh, my God, we are doomed!"

The whole village went to the King, including all the puṅḍits and brāhmaṇa priests, and said, "Aruna, Oh King, you are such a gracious and loving, generous and wise father to your children. What are we to do? The duty of the King is to protect the citizens. Yet here is your son, the heir to the throne, stealing away a brāhmaṇa girl on the day of her wedding. We want justice! Who is going to protect us if the King doesn't? Your son is the culprit! What a horrible fate to have our girl stolen away on the day of her wedding!"

The King called Satyavrat. "Satyavrat, what have you to say for yourself?"

Satyavrat replied, "Father, it wasn't all that bad."

"Why not?"

"Well, according to Hindu law, the marriage is not complete until the bride and groom have taken seven steps around the fire. Seeing as they hadn't take the seven steps yet, I am not guilty of stealing the bride. According to our Hindu law, she wasn't married."

"King, this will not do," the brāhmaṇas complained.

The King turned to his Guru, Vasiṣṭha, and asked, "Oh Respected Guru, what should be done for the peace and harmony of my kingdom?"

Vasiṣṭha thought for a moment and said, "King, having a son who causes difficulties to your subjects is worse than having no son at all. Exile the son to the forest!"

Under orders from the King, Satyavrat was exiled to the forest. Satyavrat sat alone in the forest under a tree and thought, "Am I really so unworthy that my father would throw me out of the kingdom? I can't even go home. Now I have no father. I have no mother. I have no friends. I have nothing to eat. What am I going to do out here by myself? I don't know how to do pūjā. I don't know how to do jāpa. I don't know any mantras. I don't know anything about all that tapasyā stuff. But right now I am making one vow: I am going to really be Satyavrat. I will speak the truth and I will do what I say."

Satyavrat began to live in the forest. He made a bow and some arrows and used them to hunt in the woods. In this way he forgot all about the kingdom. And he never told a lie. He lived very simply in the forest amidst nature, just taking the minimum necessities of life.

Some years passed. Then came a great famine. There was drought in the entire land. Viśvāmitra's wife was alone in the hermitage with all their children, while her husband was away in another land deep in meditation. As the days of drought and famine went on, she saw her children crying out because of hunger. She thought, "What am I to do? First, I was living peacefully in this aśrama with my children. My husband was off meditating, and I could pick fruits and herbs from the forest. With that I could feed my family. But now there are no more fruits and herbs in the forest. My children are crying out in hunger. What shall I do? I have no choice but to sell one of my sons. If I get some money, I'll take that money and feed the other children."

With that resolve, she took a rope and put it around her son's neck and started to lead him to the market place. The child was crying, and the mother also was sad. Just as they were approaching the edge of the forest, Satyavrat saw this pitiful sight and said, "Lady, what are you doing? Why is your son crying like that?"

The muni's wife replied, "Oh Prince, we have nothing to eat, and we have no money. My children are crying out for want of food, so I have determined to sell this one son so I can feed the other children."

Satyavrat said, "Oh Lady, that is a terrible thing to do. Please don't do this! Go back to your aśrama. I am a hunter, and every day I'll put some meat on the tree outside your aśrama. You can cook the meat and feed your family. Every day I will provide you something. This is my vow. I am Satyavrat, one who is truthful to his vows."

Viśvāmitra's wife was ecstatic with joy. She took the rope off her son's neck and led him back to the aśrama. Every day Satyavrat would hunt in the forest, and he would find a rabbit or a bird or some kind of animal. He would shoot the animal with his arrows and cut off a piece of meat for himself, and the rest he would hang from the tree outside the muni's aśrama. And every day Viśvāmitra's wife would come to the tree, where she would find a piece of meat. She would take it down and prepare it and cook it to feed to her children. In this way, a long period passed. But still it didn't rain.

One day, Satyavrat didn't find any game in the forest. He searched the entire forest, but he couldn't find anything. He thought, "What should I do? Should I give her a piece of my own flesh to eat? I have a vow to provide her with something to eat. How can I forsake my vow?"

Just as he was thinking about this, he looked over in a thicket and saw there was a cow. Not only was it a cow, but the cow belonged to Vasiṣṭha Muni. He thought, "That cow belongs to the same Vasiṣṭha who advised my father to exile me from the kingdom! I am angry with him anyway. There's a cow and I need to give some meat to the muni's wife!"

He took his arrow and without further thought, he shot the cow. He cut up the meat and hung it from the tree. Viśvāmitra's wife, without thinking that it might be cow's meat, came and took the meat down from the tree. She prepared it, served it to her children, and also ate of it herself. Unknowingly, they all ate the cow's meat.

Vasiṣṭha started to look for his cow, but he didn't find her anywhere. He called and searched and looked everywhere for the cow, but he didn't find the cow at all. Then he sat down in meditation and saw that Satyavrat had killed the cow. "That no-good exiled prince! That brat of a prince who is always in trouble! He killed my cow!" Vasiṣṭha got very angry with the prince, and he took some water in the palm of his hand and said, "Satyavrat, I pronounce a curse on you! You become Triśaṅku."

Tri means the number three, and śaṅku means a mark of leprosy; Triśaṅku bears three marks of leprosy. Vasiṣṭha threw the water, which bound the curse, and immediately Triśaṅku broke out with three marks of leprosy on his forehead. He had a horrible appearance, and he was extremely pained.

"What a horrible curse of leprosy I have received," exclaimed Satyavrat. "It was really no fault of my own. I had to protect my vow by providing some meat to the muni's wife."

Triśaṅku remained in the forest. One day, he saw a wild pig being chased by a tiger, and he heared the pig cry in fright, "Ai." And Triśaṅku thought, "What kind of noise is this, Ai?" For some reason he started to repeat the same syllable Ai. Triśaṅku started to say, "Ai, Ai, Ai!" Without understanding what he was saying, or what it meant, he continued to recite the strange sound he learned from the pig.

Then one day the Goddess Sarasvatī came to him. "It's Aiṁ, you fool!" She said. "But, Triśaṅku, even still, you have been faithful to your vow, and you have not transgressed the truth. I am ready to give you a boon. What would you like from me?"

Triśaṅku said, "I want to have my beautiful body back and get rid of this leprosy. I want my father to give me my kingdom back, and I don't want to be an outcast living alone in the forest anymore."

Sarasvatī said, "Tatā-stu, I grant you that boon. Even now your father's ministers are on the way to come to find you."

Sarasvatī disappeared and Triśaṅku began to shine with his beautiful appearance again. Just then the King's ministers found the prince in the forest. They said, "Oh Prince, your father has been so anxious for you. Please come home."

In the forest Satyavrata heard a pig make the squeeling noise, "Ai," and he, too, began to repeat the sound "Ai."

Even being only a portion of the bījā mantra of Saraswati, without the anusvara 'ṁ,' and having received the mantra with no explanation, with no understanding, with no instruction, with no meaning, with no Ṛṣi, Chandas, or Devatā, without a meditation, or a nyāsa, or any system of worship or discipline, without proper spelling, without "Correct" pronunciation, and that, too, having been initiated by a wild pig in the forest, even so, Satyavrata received the blessing from the Goddess.

If Satyavrata could have reached to that great attainment under such circumstances, what about the pure devotees who are consciously striving in the path of self-realization, who have received a mantra from someone they respect very highly, a qualified Guru, in a pure ceremony of worship, conducted according to scripturally ordained rites, in a pure place, with full intention, and trying to the extent of their capacity to practice spiritual discipline according to the traditions of the learned, and trying to pronounce according to their capacity of understanding, while understanding the meaning, why should they be concerned that a mistake in pronunciation could bring them harm?

And the text goes on to state that in the assemblies of the learned there are many examples of such occurances, of individuals attaining their desired goal, even without proper pronunciation.

Deva Datta asked Gobhila to continue the story.

The prince, Satyavrat, was pleased to return with the ministers.

When Triśaṅku/Satyavrat came to the edge of the kingdom, his father rode out of the city to greet him. He said, "My son, I have been so concerned about you. My time has come to go to the forest to perform tapasyā. Now you take charge of the kingdom. I am going to perform the spiritual discipline by which I can ascend to my heavenly abode."

So Satyavrat was crowned the King, and he began to reign over his kingdom.

One day, Satyavrat went to the Guru Vasiṣṭha, and said, "Guruji, Vasiṣṭha Muni, please perform the sacrfice by which I, too, can ascend to heaven."

Vasiṣṭha said, "That is not possible. You were a brat as a child. You were always in trouble; you disobeyed; you stole a brāhmaṇa's wife; you killed my cow; you are a sinner, and you can't go to heaven. Especially not right now."

"Why can't I go to heaven now?"

"No one can go to heaven with an earthly body. So if you behave yourself for the rest of your life and don't sin anymore, then we can perform a sacrifice for you, so that after you leave this earthly body, you can go to heaven. But the body will have to stay here. No one can take their body to heaven."

Satyavrat again requested, "Mahā Ṛṣi, Guruji, Great Wise One: you know all of the sacrifices. Why don't you perform the sacrifice so I can go to heaven right now?"

Vasiṣṭha again replied, "I already told you that it is impossible! Nobody can go to heaven with their body right now. Wait until you leave this body and then maybe you can go to heaven if your karma is perfect."

Satyavrat said, "Guruji, you're just picking on me! You didn't like me from my childhood. It was you who advised my father to exile me from the kingdom! It was you who cursed me to become afflicted with leprosy! If you don't do this sacrifice for me right now, then I'll have to find another guru who will do it for me. But I want to go to heaven with my body now!"

Vasiṣṭha said, "You were a foolish child and nothing has changed at all. Now you are behaving like a cāṇḍālā, an outcast, and I curse you! You shall become a cāṇḍālā!" Vasiṣṭha took some water in his hand, and threw it at Satyavrat.

Immediately, the crown fell from his head. Satyavrat's golden ornaments fell off, his silken robes became tattered rags, and he became most wretched and decrepit. He said, "Oh my gosh, I am doomed! I can't let my subjects see me like this. What a disgrace!"

Satyavrat had one son named Hariścandra. He called his young son, Hariścandra, and said, "Son, see the terrible condition that has afflicted me. You take over the leadership of the affairs of state. I am going to the forest to perform Prayaścitta, the tapasyā of repentence. I will try to find some way to relieve this terrible condition."

Satyavrat Goes to Heaven

Hariścandra was crowned as the King. Satyavrat, Triśaṅku, now suffering in a deplorable condition, went to the forest in great sorrow and pain.

Some years passed. Viśvāmitra returned to his hermitage after practicing tapasyā. When he saw his wife, his heart melted. He said, "My wife, tell me how you passed the days of the drought and famine? How did you survive? I, myself, was striken with a terrible condition. At one time I found myself so hungry, I broke into the house of a cāṇḍālā. I went directly into his kitchen, where I saw a little bit of leftovers of some dog meat he had cooked some days before. I reached into the pot to eat it. Just then the cāṇḍālā came home. He said, 'Oh Brāhmaṇa, what are you about to do?'

"And I replied, 'I am in great pain from my hunger, so I am going to steal this dog meat from a cāṇḍālā, and eat it, so that I can save my body!'

"The cāṇḍālā said, 'Oh Brāhmaṇa, learned that you are, please stop! Don't do that. My life is defiled. I am unclean. I am unworthy to provide food for a brāhmaṇa. The pots and utensils are unclean, the meat itself is unclean. It is not befitting a brāhmaṇa. Please, don't eat defiled food, because it is written, 'He who eats defiled food, becomes defiled himself'. Don't sacrifice your noble birth as a brāhmaṇa to become a cāṇḍālā in your next life!'

"Again I replied, 'My first obligation is to preserve my life. Because this human life gives me the opportunity to perform the sādhana, the spiritual discipline, by which God-Realization is obtained, I am required to protect my life. If I commit any offense in doing so, then I can always perform some tapasyā of repentence. But if I allow this human life to slip through my fingers, before my goal of Perfection of Realization is reached, then I will be guilty of a greater crime.'

"The cāṇḍālā said, 'Oh Noble Brāhmaṇa, be that as it may. I am requesting you, please don't commit this sin of stealing defiled meat from a defiled being and eating the dog meat of a cāṇḍālā. Surely the Gods will help you in your plight.'

"Again I replied, 'I cannot wait any longer for the Gods to help me. I am very disturbed by these pangs of hunger. Now, I must take some nourishment for this body! I will eat the meat!'

"Just then a bolt of lightning flew across the heavens. The clouds began to thunder and the rain fell! I put down the meat and ran outside and raised my arms up to the heavens and rejoiced! The Gods had sent rain! The drought was over! The famine was finished!

"And therefore, my dear wife, I came home to see how you and the children got along during the period of drought."

The muni's wife said, "Husband, I, too, was very perplexed by hunger. It was most pitiful to hear the cries of our children who were hungry. They kept saying, 'Mother, give us something to eat!'

"At first I gathered wild rice and grains from the forest, but then there was none. Then I gathered berries and fruits, but then they, too, were finished. Then I gathered roots, but they became exhausted as well. When the children were crying so pitifully for food, I was in such a detestable state that I didn't know what to do. Then I decided to sell one of our sons. Perhaps a rich man would purchase him, and with the proceeds of the sale, I could buy some food to keep the others alive. Just as I was in route to the market place, Satyavrat came and said, 'Oh Dear One, don't commit this horrible act. I will provide meat for your family every day so long as the famine lasts.'

"Every day I went outside the aśrama and found a piece of meat tied to the tree. But then one day, Satyavrat, killed Vasiṣṭha's cow, and Vasiṣṭha cursed him to be a cāṇḍālā. Again he was exiled from his kingdom. Now, my husband, we must do something to repay the kindness of Satyavrat."

Viśvāmitra immediately went to where Satyavrat was staying in the forest. He said, "Satyavrat, you appear to be in a detestible condition. How did you get to be like this?"

"I went to my guru and said, 'Vasiṣṭha, please perform the sacrifice by which I can ascend to heaven in this body.' And when Vasiṣṭha refused, I said, 'Vasiṣṭha, if you don't do this sacrifice for me, then I will have it performed by some other guru.' Whereupon Vasiṣṭha cursed me to become a cāṇḍālā. Now you see my pitiful condition. I can never go to heaven with this despicable body."

Viśvāmitra said, "I personally will send you to heaven, right now with this very body. You have done such a wonderful service to my family, and thereby you have become my great benefactor. I will see that you get to heaven. Bring me the articles needed for the sacrifice."

Satyavrat began to collect all the required articles and he brought them to the sacrificial altar. Viśvāmitra invited all the other munis, "Come to the Sacrifice!"

But Vasiṣṭha ordered them, "Don't anybody go!"

And no munis would disobey Vasiṣṭha's order.

Then Viśvāmitra said, "Satyavrat, sit by the sacrificial altar. We will make this sacrifice by ourselves!"

Satyavrat sat down, while Viśvāmitra enkindled the sacred fire. He began to recite the mantras and he said, "Go up, Satyavrat. Go to heaven!"

Immediately, Satyavrat lifted off the earth and began to ascend to the heavens. He moved up, up, up through the clouds, through the atmosphere, and he moved towards the heavens. Some of the Gods were sitting near the door of heaven and said, "Indra! Look at that cāṇḍālā, that outcast. That defiled being is coming up to heaven!"

Indra came running to the gate and said, "Satyavrat! Triśaṅku in a cāṇḍālā form! What are you doing here? Go back to earth! No cāṇḍālā can come through the gate of heaven!"

And Satyavrat started to fall. He fell through the clouds, and as he approached the earth, he started screaming, "Viśvāmitra! Viśvāmitra! Save me! Save me! I'm falling!"

And Viśvāmitra called out, "Stop! I sent you to heaven! No one has the authority to disallow you! Go back to heaven!"

Immediately Triśaṅku began to rise into the air. As he pushed through the clouds, he came near to the gate of heaven, and Indra said, "What are you doing back here? I sent you to earth. Go back!"

Again Satyavrat started to fall. Then Viśvāmitra said, "Stop!"

And Indra said, "Stop!"

There was Satyavrat, stuck in the atmosphere halfway between heaven and earth. He could neither go up, nor could he go down. He was stuck in the middle.

Viśvāmitra said, "Indra! You take this man to heaven."

Indra said, "He is a cāṇḍālā, an outcast, in a despicable body. There is no way he is coming to heaven! You take him back to earth."

In great anger Viśvāmitra replied, "All right, we'll see about this!"

He began to recite the Gāyatrī mantra, and made offerings to the sacred fire and said, "All the merits which I have obtained from all the tapasyā that I have performed, I give to Triśaṅku! Now Triśaṅku, go to heaven."

Indra said, "He can't come in!"

Viśvāmitra began to chant the Gāyatrī mantra once again. "What are you doing?" asked Indra.

Viśvāmitra replied, "I am making a new creation, with a new heaven and a new Indra! If Satyavrat is not welcome in your heaven, then I will send him to that heaven."

Indra said, "Stop! We don't need another creation. I don't want another heaven with another Indra. I'll allow Satyavrat into this heaven. But not with that body. Let him have a divine body, and then he can enter."

There in the middle of the atmosphere where Satyavrat was suspended, he suddenly became endowed with a beautiful, healthy divine body. He was dressed in silken garments and golden ornaments. Indra sent the Devas with a chariot that flies through the air, and Satyavrat sat down as they escorted him up to Indra's heaven. Indra gave him a place in heaven, because of the strength of Viśvāmitra's tapasyā.

The Merchant's Devoted Servant

There was a very wealthy merchant who had a very devoted servant. This servant was very much trusted by his master and had great respect for his employer. This servant had full faith that all that the master had attained in life was from the blessings from his guru.

Whenever the master's guru would come as a guest to the employer's home, this servant would volunteer to perform all of the guru's personal services. He would wash his clothes, rub his feet, see about his food, perform the guru's errands.

He said to himself, "I must try my best to get as close to this guru as possible. Maybe he will bless me, too."

One day he asked the guru, "Guruji, would you please give me the mantra that you gave my master, by which he became so successful. May I have initiation from you?"

The guru replied, "Next time."

The simple servant was so joyously grateful, and he went into his room, closed the door, and didn't come out.

Some months later the guru returned to the master's house. The master came running out to meet the guru and said, "Guruji, what did you do to my servant?"

Guruji said, "I didn't do anything to your servant. What is the problem?"

"Guruji, ever since you were here last time, you must have said something to that servant. He went into his room that day and closed the door, and I haven't seen him since."

"That can't be," replied the guru. "He asked me for initiation and I said, 'Next time.'"

"Well, Guruji, I haven't seen him since you left. He has been inside of his room, and he won't come out."

The guru said, "I shall see into this matter." He went to the servant's room and opened up the door. There he saw the faithful servant sitting in his āsana, lost in deep meditation, repeating the mantra, "Next time, next time."

Now this is what our traditions teach us: that devotion and intention are much more powerful than technique and inflection. From where did these notions of a right way or a wrong way come? What is the origin of these differences?

Brahmā's Yajña and Dakṣa's Curse

Brahmā was performing a great sacrifice, to which Śiva and Satī were invited to attend. When Dakṣa walked into the hall of sacrifice, everyone in the room stood up to greet him. They all bowed with clasped hands: "Namaste, Dakṣa Prajāpati. With all of the Energy of Consciousness we bow to the divinity manifest within you. Namaste. Your tapasyā has been victorious! You are shining radiantly and we know you are the one who made the Divine Mother take birth in your house. Prajāpati, you are the Pati, the Lord, of all Prajā, all beings born, the Lord of all beings."

Everybody stood up to show their respect. Only Brahmā and Śiva remained seated. Then Dakṣa thought, "Brahmā is my father, and there is no reason for him to stand up to greet his son. But everyone in the three worlds has stood up to pay me honor and respect, except Śiva. And he is my son-in-law. What kind of impudence is this? I can understand my father not standing up, but my son-in-law? I'm mad!"

Dakṣa walked over to Śiva and said, "Śiva, you no good uncouth, foul-behaviored person. You are the lowest of the low. You hang around with ghosts and goblins, you are always taking intoxicants. Now you are showing such disrespect to me? Śiva, I curse you! You live without a house and without a roof, and your devotees will be just like you. They will all be beggars, they will all be penniless, they will all be stoned freaks and hippies, every one of them. They will take intoxicants. They won't know how to pronounce Saṁskṛt correctly! That's the kind of devotees you will have!" And he took some water and threw it at Śiva. Śiva just sat there, and didn't react at all.

Nandi's Curse

Now Śiva's friend and chief disciple is a devotee named Nandi, the bull. Nandi could not stand this outrage and insult to his Lord. He came over and explained, "Hey Dakṣa, do you know who you're talking to? This is not an ordinary hippie to whom you speak. This is not just one of the sādhus, nor just any one of the Gods. This is Mahādeva! The Deva of the devas, God of the Gods. He is the highest, the Consciousness of Infinite Goodness. He is the Supreme Consciousness, the Guru of all gurus.

"He didn't refrain from touching your feet out of disrespect. He did it because he didn't want anything bad to happen to you. Everybody knows that if someone who is very high touches the feet of someone who is very low, obviously something very bad is going to happen. He was trying to save you that disgrace. And now you see, he is so pure and free from anger, he has accepted your curse without reply. He didn't even utter one word back to you.

"I am a devotee of Śiva. I am not Śiva. I am not as self-controlled as Śiva, and when you cursed my Lord that way, I cannot help but to curse you back. Dakṣa, your followers may pronounce Saṁskṛt correctly, but they won't understand a word they are saying. They will preach the letter of the law, but they won't understand the spirit. They will sell their dharma, and they will do their pūjās only for money. They will all be well fed, well clothed and well housed; but their homes and their hearts will be empty. They will make a show of their faith to earn money. Even if they pronounce the mantras correctly, they won't understand what they are saying. And that's the curse I give to you!" Nandi threw some Gaṅgā water at him.

Dakṣa turned around and stormed out of the house. He went home saying, "I will show that Śiva, I will fix him!"

Śivapurāna, Rudrasaṁhitā, Chapter 26

And then he began preparations to perform Dakṣa's Yajna.

We all know what happened then. But that is not the focus of our story. The important part is that Dakṣa cursed Śiva that his followers won't know how to pronounce Saṁskṛt correctly, and Nandi cursed Dakṣa that even if his followers pronounce the mantras correctly, they won't understand what they are saying!

Today there are three types of sādhus:

the followers of Śiva, who may not know how to pronounce Saṁskṛt correctly;

the followers of Dakṣa, who may pronounce Saṁskṛt correctly, but don't understand what they are saying;

and the third is a category of pure devotees, who neither know how to pronounce correctly, nor understand what it is that they are saying, but just believe in God, and have faith that by following the path of the Ṛṣis, by reciting what the Ṛṣis recited as closely as they can to the way the Ṛṣis recited it, these devotees, too, can attain to the same realization that the Ṛṣis did.

The Puṅḍit could not help noticing the illiterate farmer sitting in the back of the temple crying all throughout his learned discourse. When he was done speaking and all the congregation left except this farmer, the Puṅḍit went up to him and said, "My Friend, much of my discourse was quoting from ancient Saṁskṛt scriptures. I am sure that you could not understand my meanings. Yet you were moved to tears all throughout the discourse. How is it that even while not understanding what I was saying, you were moved to such emotion that made you cry?"

The simple farmer replied, "Oh Greatly Learned Puṅḍit, it is true that I could not understand the meanings of your words. But as you spoke I heard the name of Kriṣṇa, and I saw Him sitting on His chariot giving the discourse to Arjuna. That is what moved me to tears. I felt I was in the presence of God!"

Pronunciation and the Chaṇḍi Sampuṭs

Chandragupta Maurya was the disciple of Chanakya, a great sādhu and teacher of economics and political science. Under his guru's instructions, Chandragupta was able to unite all of India, and put an end to the Greek rule left in place by the conquering Alexander. This was around the time period of 323 BCE.

After the kingdom was unified, Chanakya had a great university constructed at Pātaliputra, and under his direction, an army of scholars was sent about the various parts of the empire to collect the traditions from each community, and to write them down in one script, Devanagri. These manuscripts were organized in a great library in the university at Pātaliputra. Prior to this, the traditions were mostly oral, or at best, written down in the local language scripts.

In 639 AD, Sron-btsan sgam-po, a king from Southern Tibet, conquered all of Tibet, annexed Nepal, established Lhasa as his capital city, and made it rich as the crossroads of trade between India and China. He invited Buddhist monks from India to spread education among his people, and even sent Thon-mi Sambhota, one of his ministers and best friend, to India to devise a script for the Tibetan language based on Devanagri. Thousands of monasteries were built in the mountains and on the great plateau, which housed voluminous libraries translated or transliterated from Pāli and Saṁskṛt scriptures. The king himself took off four years from administration in order to study, became adept at reading and writing, and thus began a Golden Age of Tibet, which lasted for a full one hundred fifty years.

In 1008 Mahmud Ghaznavi from South-eastern Afghanistan, crossed over the Khyber Pass into India, plundered the wealth stored in the temples, and became one of the most admired among the Islamic Potentates. Then came the Turks, the Huns, various tribes rose against each other, and by 1206 the Islamic Sultanate of Delhi was the supreme ruling authority. History will attest that from Attila the Hun, Tamerlane, Babur, Humayan, all the way to Aurangzeb, there seemed to be a competition to demonstrate how much non-Islamic culture could be destroyed. Everywhere fundamentalist Islamic forces occupied a defeated nation, there was a mandate to eradicate all culture and history that was pre-Islamic. Whether it was the sculptures of Babylonia, the libraries of Alexandria and Heliopolis, the temples of Jerusalem, everywhere Islam invaded, they devastated the existing cultures and made Islam the predominant religion.

They converted temples into mosques, burned whole libraries of books, defaced sculptures, killed the priests, and offered conversion to Islam, the religion of peace, as a salvation for defeated populations. All across the north of India, all of "Hindustan," wherever Moslem rule extended, temples were either destroyed or converted to mosques, statues were defaced, and the non-Islamic cultures subjugated to the ruling ideals. Whether it be Ayodhya or Mathura or Benaris, no sanctuary of non-Islamic culture was exempt. Where Hindus worshipped God with art, Islam proclaimed that any representation of divinity is sacrilegious, and therefore the most religious people in Islam are those who destroy the idolatry of the non-believers.

Even in our own era, the Taliban of Afghanistan decimated the Buddhist rock sculptures of Bamiyan, plundered the Museum of Archeology in Kabul, and then publicly sacrificed a cow from every district of the country in order to atone for the sin of having lived in a land populated by foreign idolators.

It was the year 1600 when the British founded the East India Company, and 1690 when they moved to Calcutta. The British business model was exactly opposite to that of the Greeks. Whereas Alexander conquered India by aiding one king against another, until there was no one left to oppose him, the British sold "Protection." With a trained and disciplined army and superior fire power, the British hired themselves out to the Kings and Sultans, in an arrangement to discourage others from attacking their holdings. Being employed by all parties to every dispute, it took only a short time before they gained the upper hand in guarantying safety, and by 1858 the British Crown took over the entire country.

So first came the adventurers, then the explorers, then businessmen, and then the missionaries. Then came the army, and lastly the politicians. It was with the missionaries that Saṁskṛt became recognized as a key to ancient history, and the sciences of philology and ethnology became established. In 1805 Colbrooke wrote an essay on the Vedas, and about the same time, Anquetil-Duperron translated from a Persian translation of the Upanishads into German. This had a profound influence on Schelling and Schopenhauer. Burnouf in France wrote Essays on Pāli, and his student was Max Mueller, of German decent, living at the center of education in the civilized world at Oxford in England, who undertook to publish his edited compilation of the Rig Veda in Saṁskṛt, and to compile a series called, "The Sacred Books of the Ancient East."

His first edition of the first volume of the Rig Veda was published in October, 1849, at Oxford. At that time only those with British scholastic credentials were considered to be educated. Sir Williams Jones, Sir Edwin Arnold, Sir John Woodroffe, Griffith, Whitehead, Williams, MacDonald, all became authorities over Saṁskṛt literature. Just as the Indians were not competent to write their own histories, in the same way they were no longer empowered to be authorities over their own literature, their scriptures, or their religious heritage. It was Swami Vivekananda who, in 1893, astounded the West by being the first Indian who could speak eloquently about his religion and philosophy without a foreign diploma.

These books by foreign scholars were so expensive to print, that most of the people who could afford to buy them, had no capacity to read them. Most could not read the Devanagri script. So the issue of transliteration arose. Sir Charles Trevelyan had inaugurated the process in 1834 in Calcutta. Soon he was joined by other scholars from the Royal Asiatic Society, as well as the Church Missionary Society, at the Congress of Orientalists held in Berlin in September, 1881. But it took until the Transliteration Committee of the Geneva Oriental Congress, in September, 1894, to reach an agreement.

It is easy to see how the negotiations were conducted. Take, for example, the anusvara, 'ṁ'. In the North it is generally pronounced as a nasal 'n'. In the South it is often pronounced as a hard 'm'. In the East it is most frequently pronounced as 'ng'. The Church Missionary Society was most active in the South, and therefore, the anusvara was represented by 'ṁ'.

Let us take the 'ai' sound. In the North it is generally pronounced as 'aye' or ai as in aisle. In the South it is often pronounced as 'ei'. In the East it is most frequently pronounced as 'oi'. The Northern pronunciation won out for the Transliteration Committee, but each region still maintains its own individual sounds and modes of pronunciation.

Monier Williams relied on this system of transliteration for his monumental dictionary, published at Oxford in 1899. His dictionary is still the definitive authority in English on Saṁskṛt to this day, even though it appears in Roman letters, and was compiled by individuals foreign to the culture. But because the western scholars were by in large academics and not practitioners, their works, no matter how helpful to future scholars, contain a number of inconsistent definitions, misinterpretations, and faulty applications. For example, in many translations of the Rig Veda, the Aryan Ṛṣis are often shown as praying for cows, from the root, "Go". Mr. Williams' dictionary shows that "Go" means cows or cattle, and "Go" means rays of light. Some translators wanted to maintain consistency, so "Go" always meant cows. "Gopala" the protector of cows works very well, and the Gopis are the cow-herding girls. But Gauri is known as a Goddess, rather than "She Who is Rays of Light". Govinda should be "He Who is one-pointed in the light".

Nevertheless, the task of organizing Saṁskṛt literature was appropriated by Western scholars. Because the North of India had been dominated and decimated by Islam for at least a few hundred years, if not many more, these scholars relied heavily upon their teams of advisors from all over the Indian Continent. Once again scriptures were collected from every source, from every language, and added to whatever remnants could be found of the North Indian Saṁskṛt traditions.

This exercise yielded a number of variations for each scripture. The Bhagavad Gītā specifically states that it contains 700 verses, but the versions we find in print today contain 738 verses. Which verses are unauthorized? It is impossible to say.

Pronunciation and the Chaṇḍi Samputs

In the Chaṇḍi Pāṭh there are a number of inconsistencies. For example, in Chapter 11, verse 7 alternatively says:

sarva bhūtā yadā devī svarga mukti pradāyinī |

or

sarva bhūtā yadā devī svarga bhukti pradāyinī |

Verse 22 alternatively says:

mahārātri mahāmāye nārāyaṇi namo-stu te ||

or

mahārātre mahāvidye nārāyaṇi namo-stu te ||

Verse 34 alternatively says:

pāpāni sarva jagatāṁ praśamaṁ nayāśu

or

pāpāni sarva jagatāṁ ca śāmaṁ nayāśu

And we can find numerous other examples. Which is the "Correct" version? It is difficult to say. Does it make any difference? Not significantly. There are slight changes in the meaning, but they are minor changes in comparison with the overall understanding of the Chaṇḍi Pāṭh. And this is true of the other scriptures as well. The main point is that as these traditions were written down, transcribed from many sources, from many languages, and from many alphabets, once under Chanakya, again under the guidance of the Tibetans or Tamils, and various others, there were several interpolations, several deviations, from one version to the next.

Saṁskṛt is commonly taught with fifty letters, sixteen vowels and thirty-four consonants. Occasionally it is taught with fifty-two letters, with the addition of oṁ and hrīṁ. Alternatively, it is taught with fifty-four letters with the inclusion of tra and jña.

However the languages from which they were translating and transliterating to and from, contain various numbers of characters. 'Authentic' Tamil has 12 vowels and 18 consonants. In order to adapt for some Saṁskṛt/North Indian letters, 5 extra consonants have been added, making the total number of consonants 23, a maximum of thirty-five characters. In Tamil there is only one consonant 'K', which is both K and G. There are no characters for Kh and Gh.

The Tibetan alphabet contains forty characters. Of the five vowels, a is included with every consonant, but the other four: i, u, e, and o are diacritical characters. There are thirty consonants, plus five extra used for writing Saṁskṛt. There are 90 conjunct consonants, each of which forms a different character.

Telugu has 48 letters, 14 vowels and 34 consonants
Kannada has 48 letters, 14 vowels and 34 consonants
Malayalam has 50 letters, 13 vowels and 37 consonants
Gujarati has 46 letters, 12 vowels and 34 consonants
Punjabi has 42 letters, 10 vowels and 32 consonants
Bengali has 43 letters, 11 vowels and 32 consonants, and at least 42 conjunct consonants, each of which forms a different character.

And of course, English or Roman has 26 characters.

And not only are the numbers of characters different in every script, but the pronunciation of each character varies significantly from script to script, and from region to region.

India has sixteen major languages officially recognized by the government. Each has its own script, and the number and names of the characters in each script are different. In addition there are 398 dialects officially recognized, of which 387 are called "Living languages," and 11 are extinct. And the letters are pronounced differently in each language, and again in each region in which the same language is spoken.

But every individual in every region understands that he or she is pronouncing correctly. Why not? Is it not their "Mother language?" Is it not pronounced using the alphabets they have learned from childhood? Are not all the teachers in every recognized institution of that locality pronouncing in the same way? Are not all the puṅḍits and learned men, all the respected people of that locality, pronouncing in the same way?

Herein lies the crux of the issue: the xenophobia of a heritage that presupposes that if all the teachers, puṅḍits, learned men, all the respected people of a locality are pronouncing in a certain way, it must be the right way. Without having travelled to distant temples in far off lands, without having traversed the length and breadth of India, or even visited sanctuaries of the same traditions in other countries, (Hinduism is a global culture), people assume that the scholars of their immediate community are the finest authorities, and that all others have got it wrong.

This is the major fallacy which we must understand and overcome. By understanding it's cause, we can think of what can be done to rectify the situation.

Certainly we are not suggesting that anyone should speak or recite in any way that they feel motivated or inspired. Sounds become words when they are consistent. Words become sounds when they are inconsistent. There must some consistency to the pronunciation in order to communicate meaning.

However, if we are singing from our hearts for the purpose of sincere prayer, and if we know what we are saying and why we are saying it, and others who hear our prayers can also understand their meanings, and they also become inspired to pray themselves, then we are doing it correctly. Intention, motivation, sincerity, attention, bhāva, and understanding, all go together to make a proper presentation.

The rest of us are all students!

Intention and motivation ask why are we doing this? Why are we chanting these mantras? Are we professionals who, for a fee, will propitiate the Gods so that our benefactors will not receive the fruit of their karma? In the Chaṇḍi Pāṭh, Brahmā, Vaśiṣṭha, and Viśvamitra, joined others in cursing the recitation of the Chaṇḍi performed with selfish motivation. They said that the Chaṇḍi Pāṭh is a very pure and powerful tool of personal growth and transformation. It is a path to self-realization. "Whoever will recite the Chaṇḍi Pāṭh for selfish motivation will have abused their tool, and the tool will no longer work for them."

Without the tools, the curse is equivalent to a lifetime without God. If we abuse our tools they won't work. If we think that by our recitation and prayer, we will change the karma of others, then how will we change our own? If we make a business of our spirituality, then how will we seek salvation?

So intention and motivation set the stage for the actions we are to perform. They are most important.

Next come sincerity and attention. The sincerity of our devotion is what determines its intensity. Intensity is the measurement of the sincerity of devotion. We pay attention in direct relation to the amount of devotion we feel, and feel to express. Sometimes we feel devotion, but cannot express it. Sometimes we want to express devotion that we do not feel. Other times it comes from the heart, and is expressed in the most pure means, according to the capacity of the individual.

Sādhana teaches us to express that feeling in a regular program of spiritual discipline. After practice, when we sit to create the expression, we automatically feel the sincerity.

Bhāva means feeling, emotion, an intensity of reality. How intensely do we feel it? How real is it to us when we are doing it? Is this our reality? Or is it merely a passing thought? Bhāva allows us to "Grok" the feeling, to intuit the feeling, to unite with the feeling, to be at-one-ness with the feeling, to attune to the feeling, until it is ours.

Understanding means we understand what we are saying. It is not just on a verbal level, but we know verbally and non-verbally. It means something to us. In fact, it means a lot to us.

And not just to us. But anyone who hears what we are saying will also be able to understand at least on some level the meaning of our prayer. They will know that we are praying, and may feel moved to pray themselves. They will become inspired to enter our prayer, and there is a transference of energy which invites them into the mystery of worship.

And these are the constituent elements which all go together to make a "Proper" presentation. Because "Proper" is in Her eyes, not in anyone else's.

These are the major fallacies which we must understand and overcome: instead of arguing over how it is being said, seekers should be contemplating what is being said. This has become so much misunderstood that some people may say: "If you don't do it right, it is worse than not doing it at all."

Instead we must practice to appreciate each individual's intention and endeavor, to respect the sincerity of each individual's search, to take inspiration from their efforts, and to seek understanding as to how we might implement such a program of practice in our own lives. This is the dharma of the present age, the highest ideal of perfection.

How did we move so far from these ideals is, itself, quite exemplary. It was the curse of Gautam Muni which made us all stray.

Gautam Muni and the Curse of the Brāhmaṇas

There was a time when there was a drought throughout India and everyone was wanting for water. So Gautam Muni and Ahālya, his wife, went to the summit of the Brahmāgiri Mountain to perform tapasyā. They did penance for Varuṇa on the top of that mountain. After several years of tapasyā, Varuṇa came and said, "I am going to give you a blessing. I will give you a cave from which will flow a constant source of water. And this supply of water will be eternal and will give nourishment to the entire population."

And that's just what happened. Varuṇa gave his blessing, and Gautam and Ahālya dug a cavern into the mountain and the water gushed out, and it never went dry.

Gautam and Ahālya were worshipping the Divine Mother in the form of Gāyatrī Devī, and they never experienced any lack. Some of the brāhmaṇas began to think, "Our children are crying for want of food. Our crops are whithering for want of water. Our cattle are wasting for want of sustenance. Our lives are ruined for want of blessings. Gautam and Ahālya are worshipping with such devotion and they never have any lack. Let us go take refuge with them."

And that is what they did. They packed up all their belongings and their families, and went to where Gautam and Ahālya were performing constant worship. When Ṛṣi Gautam saw the brāhmaṇa families coming, he made them welcome with great respect. He prayed to the Goddess Gāyatrī, whereupon he found all the necessary means with which to welcome his guests. He gave them seats upon which to sit, and then he washed their feet, gave them new clothes, fed them wonderful food, and when they were all comfortably composed, he gave them articles for worship, and asked them all to worship the Divine Mother together. As many people as came, Gautam and Ahālya welcomed them in this way, and soon people for hundreds of miles around were worshipping the Supreme Goddess throughout the day and night.

All the citizens were so happy to have water and they were saved from the drought. Everyone was singing the praise of Gautam and Ahālya. Even the Gods in heaven were joyous upon watching their activities.

Some of the brāhmaṇas began to think, "We are brāhmaṇas and we are performing constant worship. Why is everyone singing the praise of Gautam and Ahālya? They should be acknowledging the contribution of the brāhmaṇas. If it were not for the teachers, what would the students learn, and what could they be practicing?" And silently the corrupted thinking of egotistical attachment took over their being.

One day some village boys came to draw water from the spring, and some of the brāhmaṇa ladies who were present there stopped them and said, "We are brāhmaṇas. We should take our water first."

Gautam's wife, Ahālya, happened to be there, and she said, "No, ladies, this water is for everyone. It was a gift from God to all the people. There is no one question of who goes first and who goes second; whoever comes first, gets served first. There is no idea of caste or creed here. This is God's water, which is the life of the people."

The brāhmaṇa women answered, "What is this? Ahālya has become so proud because of her tapasyā. She and her husband brought the water, and now they are giving lectures to us. We're brāhmaṇa women, and she is telling us who should go first and who should go after? She thinks it's her water and she is the only one who has authority?"

Those women went back to their village, and they went to their husbands and said, "We need to find some way to curb the pride of Gautam and Ahālya. They are just too proud of their having been the ones who brought the water that filled the cavern and saved the lives of the people."

So the brāhmaṇa men conspired on a plan. They took an old sickly cow to where Gautam was making the fire sacrifice in his Yajñaśāla. This old sick cow was just on its last legs before death, and they prodded that cow to the sacrificial area. Then they pushed the cow inside. Gautam was sitting in his āsana before the sacred fire, reciting the holy mantras of the sacrifice. He took a spoonful of ghee from his bowl, and pronounced the mantra, "*Huṁ Phaṭ Svāhā!*" Putting the ghee into the fire, he caused that fire to shoot up into the air, and just then the cow fell over and died!

All the brāhmaṇas assembled there said, "Oh my God! Ṛṣi Gautam killed that cow with his mantra! What kind of Ṛṣi is he to kill a cow? This is a terrible thing! He has sinned, he has killed the cow! It is Gohatya, the sin of killing a cow!"

Gautam became silent and went into deep meditation.

"You will have to perform great penance in order to repent for this sin," they said. "You will not be accepted among the society of brāhmaṇas until your penance is complete!"

Gautam asked, "What penance do you think is appropriate to become free from my sins? What would you have me perform?"

And the brāhmaṇas replied, "You will have to make the waters of this cave flow all the way down to us in the cities below, so we will not have to climb up the mountain to fetch water. When you make the river flow down to us, we will know that your sins have been forgiven."

So Gautam and Ahālya began to propitiate Lord Śiva in an even greater vow of penance. They performed tapasyā for twelve years, whereupon Śiva came to them and said, "I am very pleased with your sincerity, and I am giving you the boon of your desire. The river will flow down from the spring in this cave on the mountain to the cities below. She will become a mighty river, and She will travel across the breadth of India and nourish all of mankind. Because your tapasyā has brought Her, She will be known as Gautamī or Godāvarī to immortalize your penance.

Then Śiva said to Gautam, "You were not guilty of killing the cow. It was the jealousy of the brāhmaṇas, which made them conspire against you. They schemed and they conspired to push that old sickly cow into the sacrificial area to die where you were worshipping. You were not guilty."

Then Gautam became very angry with those brāhmaṇas. He took some water from the Godāvarī River in his hand and he pronounced a curse on them. He said. "I curse you brāhmaṇas because you have done such a terrible act!"

|| 56 ||

वेदमातरि गायत्र्यां तद्ध्याने तन्मनोर्जपे ।

भवताऽनुन्मुखा यूयं सर्वदा ब्राह्मणाऽधमाः ॥

vedamātari gāyatryāṁ taddhyāne tanmanorjape
bhavatā-nunmukhā yūyaṁ
sarvadā brāhmaṇā-dhamāḥ

The meditation on the Mother of the Vedas, Gāyatrī Devi, and the mental recitation of Her mantras, oh lowest of brāhmaṇas, may you always be averse to these practices, may they not show their face to you.

|| 57 ||

वेदे वेदोक्तयज्ञेषु तद्वार्तासु तथैवच ।

भवताऽनुन्मुखा यूयं सर्वदा ब्राह्मणाधमाः ॥

vede vedoktayajñeṣu tadvārtāsu tathaivaca
bhavatā-nunmukhā yūyaṁ
sarvadā brāhmaṇā-dhamāḥ

The worship and yajñas, various fire sacrifices explained in the Vedas, oh lowest of brāhmaṇas, may you always be averse to these practices, may they not show their face to you.

|| 58 ||

शिवे शिवस्य मन्त्रे च शिवशास्त्रे तथैव च ।

भवताऽनुन्मुखा यूयं सर्वदा ब्राह्मणाधमाः ॥

śive śivasya mantre ca śivaśāstre tathaiva ca
bhavatā-nunmukhā yūyaṁ
sarvadā brāhmaṇā-dhamāḥ

The study of scriptures of Śiva, recitation of the mantras of Śiva, contemplation of the names of Śiva, oh lowest of brāhmaṇas, may you always be averse to these practices, may they not show their face to you.

|| 59 ||

मूलप्रकृत्याः श्रीदेव्यास्तद्ध्याने तत्कथासु च ।

भवताऽनुन्मुखा यूयं सर्वदा ब्राह्मणाधमाः ॥

mūlaprakṛtyāḥ śrīdevyāstaddhyāne tatkathāsu ca
bhavatā-nunmukhā yūyaṁ
sarvadā brāhmaṇā-dhamāḥ

The meditation on the stories about the Primordial Nature and all the respected Gods, oh lowest of brāhmaṇas, may you always be averse to these practices, may they not show their face to you.

|| 60 ||

देवीमन्त्रे तथा देव्याः स्थानेऽनुष्ठानकर्मणि ।

भवताऽनुन्मुखा यूयं सर्वदा ब्राह्मणाधमाः ॥

devīmantre tathā devyāḥ
sthāne-nuṣṭhānakarmaṇi
bhavatā-nunmukhā yūyaṁ
sarvadā brāhmaṇā-dhamāḥ

The activities of Purifying Austerities with the mantras of the Goddess in any place where the Gods are worshipped, oh lowest of brāhmaṇas, may you always be averse to these practices, may they not show their face to you.

|| 61 ||

देव्युत्सवदिद्दक्षायां देवीनामानुकीर्तने ।

भवताऽनुन्मुखा यूयं सर्वदा ब्राह्मणाधमाः ॥

devyutsavadiddakṣāyāṁ devīnāmānukīrtane
bhavatā-nunmukhā yūyaṁ
sarvadā brāhmaṇā-dhamāḥ

Celebrating the various festivals of the Goddess with skill and singing the names of the Goddess, oh lowest of brāhmaṇas, may you always be averse to these practices, may they not show their face to you.

|| 62 ||

देवीभक्तस्य सान्निध्ये देवी-भक्तार्चने तथा ।

भवताऽनुन्मुखा यूयं सर्वदा ब्राह्मणाधमाः ॥

devībhaktasya sānnidhye devī-bhaktārcane tathā
bhavatā-nunmukhā yūyaṁ
sarvadā brāhmaṇā-dhamāḥ

Contemplating upon the Goddess with devotion and making offerings to the Goddess with devotion, oh lowest of brāhmaṇas, may you always be averse to these practices, may they not show their face to you.

|| 63 ||

शिवोत्सवदिद्दक्षायां शिवभक्तस्य पूजने ।

भवताऽनुन्मुखा यूयं सर्वदा ब्राह्मणाधमाः ॥

śivotsavadiddakṣāyāṁ śivabhaktasya pūjane
bhavatā-nunmukhā yūyaṁ
sarvadā brāhmaṇā-dhamāḥ

Celebrating the various festivals for Śiva and worshipping Lord Śiva with devotion, oh lowest of brāhmaṇas, may you always be averse to these practices, may they not show their face to you.

|| 64 ||

रुद्राक्षे बिल्वपत्रे च तथा शुद्धे च भस्मनि ।

भवताऽनुन्मुखा यूयं सर्वदा ब्राह्मणाधमाः ॥

rudrākṣe bilvapatre ca tathā śuddhe ca bhasmani
bhavatā-nunmukhā yūyaṁ
sarvadā brāhmaṇā-dhamāḥ

Wearing rudrākṣa, offering leaves of bel, and the purity of wearing a mark of ashes, oh lowest of brāhmaṇas, may you always be averse to these practices, may they not show their face to you.

|| 65 ||

श्रौतस्मार्तसदाचारे ज्ञानमार्गे तथैव च ।

भवताऽनुन्मुखा यूयं सर्वदा ब्राह्मणाधमाः ॥

śrautasmārtasadācāre jñānamārge tathaiva ca
bhavatā-nunmukhā yūyaṁ
sarvadā brāhmaṇā-dhamāḥ

Remembering truthful behavior and the path of wisdom propounded in the Vedas, oh lowest of brāhmaṇas, may you always be averse to these practices, may they not show their face to you.

|| 66 ||

अद्वैतज्ञाननिष्ठायां शान्तिदान्त्यादिसाधने ।

भवताऽनुन्मुखा यूयं सर्वदा ब्राह्मणाधमाः ॥

advaitajñānaniṣṭhāyāṁ śāntidāntyādisādhane
bhavatā-nunmukhā yūyaṁ
sarvadā brāhmaṇā-dhamāḥ

The allegiance to the wisdom of non-duality, and the spiritual discipline of the greatest peace, oh lowest of brāhmaṇas, may you always be averse to these practices, may they not show their face to you.

|| 67 ||

नित्यकर्माद्यनुष्ठानेऽप्यग्निहोत्रादिसाधने ।

भवताऽनुन्मुखा यूयं सर्वदा ब्राह्मणाधमाः ॥

nityakarmādyanuṣṭhāne-pyagnihotrādisādhane
bhavatā-nunmukhā yūyaṁ
sarvadā brāhmaṇā-dhamāḥ

The spiritual disciplines of fire ceremonies, the vows of continuous worship with daily disciplines, oh lowest of brāhmaṇas, may you always be averse to these practices, may they not show their face to you.

|| 68 ||

स्वाध्यायाऽध्ययने चैव तथा प्रवचनेऽपि च ।

भवताऽनुन्मुखा यूयं सर्वदा ब्राह्मणाधमाः ॥

svādhyāyā-dhyayane caiva tathā pravacane-pi ca
bhavatā-nunmukhā yūyaṁ
sarvadā brāhmaṇā-dhamāḥ

Listening to inspiring discourses and deeply studying the knowledge of your own self, oh lowest of brāhmaṇas, may you always be averse to these practices, may they not show their face to you.

|| 69 ||

गोदानादिषु दानेषु पितृश्राद्धेषु चैव हि ।

भवताऽनुन्मुखा यूयं सर्वदा ब्राह्मणाधमाः ॥

godānādiṣu dāneṣu pitṛśrāddheṣu caiva hi
bhavatā-nunmukhā yūyaṁ
sarvadā brāhmaṇā-dhamāḥ

Giving of cows and light and other offerings of inspiration, and memorial ceremonies in honor of our ancestors, oh lowest of brāhmaṇas, may you always be averse to these practices, may they not show their face to you.

|| 70 ||

कृच्छ्रचान्द्रायणे चैव प्रायश्चित्ते तथैव च ।

भवताऽनुन्मुखा यूयं सर्वदा ब्राह्मणाधमाः ॥

kṛcchracāndrāyaṇe caiva prāyaścitte tathaiva ca
bhavatā-nunmukhā yūyaṁ
sarvadā brāhmaṇā-dhamāḥ

The performance of Purifying Austerities in repentance for inappropriate behavior like the vow of Kṛcchracāndrāyaṇa, etc., oh lowest of brāhmaṇas, may you always be averse to these practices, may they not show their face to you.

|| 71 ||

श्रीदेवीभिन्नदेवेषु श्रद्धा-भक्तिसमन्विताः ।

शङ्खचक्राघङ्किताश्च भवत ब्राह्मणाधमाः ॥

śrīdevībhinnadeveṣu śraddhā-bhaktisamanvitāḥ
śaṅkhacakrāghaṅkitāśca
bhavata brāhmaṇādhamāḥ

Ignoring the Respected Goddess, without faith or devotion in any other Gods, you will display various religious symbols like a conch or cakra, oh lowest of brāhmaṇas, let that be the way for you.

|| 72 ||

कापालिकमताऽऽसक्ता बौद्ध शास्त्ररताः सदा ॥

पाखण्डचारनिरता भवत ब्राह्मणाधमाः ॥

kāpālikamatāSsaktā bauddha śāstraratāḥ sadā
pākhaṇḍacāranirata bhavata brāhmaṇādhamāḥ

From selfish desire you will follow those who worship with skulls and those who propound scriptures eloquently. You will always follow deceivers and fakes, oh lowest of brāhmaṇas, let that be the way for you.

|| 73 ||

पितृमातृसुतभ्रातृकन्याविक्रयिणस्तथा ।

भार्याक्रियिणस्तद्वद्भवत ब्राह्मणाधमाः ॥

pitṛmātṛsutabhrātṛkanyā vikrayiṇastathā
bhāryākriyiṇastadvadbhavata brāhmaṇādhamāḥ

You will sell your fathers, mothers, sons and daughters, even your wives as well, oh lowest of brāhmaṇas, let that be the way for you.

|| 74 ||

वेदविक्रयिणस्तद्वत्तीर्थविक्रयिणस्तथा ।

धर्मविक्रयिणस्तद्वद्भवत ब्राह्मणाधमाः ॥

vedavikrayiṇastadvattīrthavikrayiṇastathā
dharmavikrayiṇastadvad
bhavata brāhmaṇādhamāḥ

You will sell the Vedic Knowledge, you will sell the places of religious pilgrimage. You will even sell Dharma, your highest ideals of perfection, oh lowest of brāhmaṇas, let that be the way for you.

|| 75 ||

पाञ्चरात्रे कामशास्त्रे तथा कापालिके मते ।

बौद्धे श्रद्धायुता यूयं भवत ब्राह्मणाधमाः ॥

pāñcarātre kāmaśāstre tathā kāpālike mate
bauddhe śraddhāyutā yūyaṁ
bhavata brāhmaṇādhamāḥ

You will maintain faith in the black magic of the vow of five nights, in the scriptures of sexual indulgence, and again in the knowledge of the path of those who worship with skulls, oh lowest of brāhmaṇas, let that be the way for you.

|| 76 ||

मातृकन्यागामिनश्च भगिनीगामिनस्तथा ।

परस्त्रीलम्पटाः सर्वे भवत ब्राह्मणाधमाः ॥

mātṛkanyāgāminaśca bhaginīgāminastathā
parastrīlampaṭāḥ sarve bhavata brāhmaṇādhamāḥ

You will go to your mothers with lust, or to your daughters or nieces as well. You will desire the wives of others, oh lowest of brāhmaṇas, let that be the way for you.

|| 77 ||

युष्माकं वंशजाताश्च स्त्रियश्च पुरुषास्तथा ।

मद्दत्तशापदग्धास्ते भविष्यन्ति भवत्समाः ॥

yuṣmākaṁ vaṁśajātāśca striyaśca puruṣāstathā
maḍattaśāpadagdhāste bhaviṣyanti bhavatsamāḥ

And this curse is not for you alone, but for all the descendants of your families, both male and female, who will be born in the future. || 78 ||

किं मया बहुनोक्तेन मूलप्रकृतिरीश्वरी ।
गायत्री परमा भूयाद्युष्मासु खलु कोपिता ॥

kiṁ mayā bahunoktena mūlaprakṛtirīśvarī
gāyatrī paramā bhūyādyuṣmāsu khalu kopitā

Because of my proclamation. May the Supreme Goddess, the Highest Primordial Nature, the Goddess Gāyatrī, always be angry with you!

अन्धकूपादिकुण्डेषु युष्माकं स्यात्सदा स्थितिः ॥

andhakūpādikuṇḍeṣu yuṣmākaṁ syātsadā sthitḥi

May you continually reside in the most darkest caverns of hell!

Ṛṣi Gautam took that water from the Gaṅga and he threw it at those brāhmaṇas. When the water of that curse hit those brāhmaṇas, they realized the gravity of the curse they had received. Forgetting the wisdom of the Vedas, forgetting the Divine Mother, forgetting all the purity of spiritual discipline, is comparable to a life-time without God, a life-time without peace, without any joy or contentment. Is there any more deleterious curse that they could have received?

Realizing this, they all fell at the feet of Gautam Ṛṣi and said, "Please forgive us. We have done a terrible act, and we beg you to pardon us. We are totally ashamed of our actions, but the delusion of attachment is too strong for anyone to resist. God made a cure for every disease in existence except for foolishness. The greatest quality of a Ṛṣi is kṣāma, forgiveness, so we beg that you forgive us for our wrongdoing."

Gautam replied, "The curse that I have given to you cannot be revoked, but because of your humility I give you a blessing:"

|| 89 ||

ततः परं कलियुगे भुवि जन्म भवेद्धि वाम् ।

मदुक्तं सर्वमेतत्तु भवेदेव न चाऽन्यथा ॥

tataḥ paraṁ kaliyuge bhuvi janma bhaveddhi vām
maduktaṁ sarvametattu bhavedeva na cā-nyathā

Just as I have spoken and not other, all of that will certainly come about. You will have to take birth during the Kali Yuga, the Age of Darkness, and this will certainly come to pass.

|| 90 ||

मच्छापस्य विमोक्षार्थं युष्माकं स्याद्ददीषणा ।

तहि सेव्यं सदा सर्वैर्गायत्रीपदपङ्कजम् ॥

macchāpasya vimokṣārthaṁ
yuṣmākaṁ syāddadīṣaṇā
tahi sevyaṁ sadā sarvair gāyatrīpadapaṅkajam

In order to be freed from this curse, you must always continually serve the lotus feet of the Respected Goddess Gāyatrī.

When all the brāhmaṇas begin to study their dharma and adhere to the dharma, then the curse will be over. When every brāhmaṇa begins to practice sādhana, and live in accordance with his or her spiritual discipline, when they start to worship God for the love of God and not as a profession, then the curse will be revoked. When every brāhmaṇa chants the Gāyatrī Mantra, makes havan or ceremonial fire worship in the temples, teaches and demonstrates the highest ideals of perfection, then the curse will be over."

The brāhmaṇas were very happy to have a way to be free from the curse, and to not have to experience its fruits immediately.

But this curse is what we are experiencing today, the plight of our Hindu dharma today. When the teachers don't know their subject, what will they teach to their students? Who knows a subject can teach about the subject they know. That is the purpose and the dharma of a brāhmaṇa.

There are six karmas that are allowed to a brāhmaṇa: to learn and to teach, to worship for yourself and to worship for others, to pray for others and to lead others in worship, to give what one can and to accept offerings that are given as a token of love and respect. These are the six karmas that are allowed to a brāhmaṇa.

In the Eighteenth Chapter of the Bhagavad Gītā it says:

|| 42 ||

शमो दमस्तपः शौचं क्षान्तिरार्जवमेव च ।

ज्ञानं विज्ञानमास्तिक्यं ब्रह्मकर्म स्वभावजम् ॥

śamo damastapaḥ śaucaṁ kṣāntirārjavameva ca
jñānaṁ vijñānamāstikyaṁ
brāhmakarma svabhāvajam

Peacefulness, self-control, austerity, purity, patience, the purification of knowledge, wisdom, the application of wisdom, and the continuous pursuit of self-realization are the actions natural to a brāhmaṇa.

So our duty as members of the Sanātan Dharma is to wake up the brāhmaṇas and request them all to please remember their dharma, the highest ideals of perfection. Our duty is to request them to demonstrate for us the qualities of a brāhmaṇa, so they will continue to inspire us to noble conduct. Our duty is to support them in their dharmic actions, but not in their laziness, to learn from them the good and useful, but to discriminate what knowledge will bring us peace and what knowledge will create greater strife and conflict. Our duty is to manifest the ideals of perfection, and the brāhmaṇas must inspire us to perform the disciplines by which that perception can be maintained.

Now the question arises as to who has authority to perform these disciplines. Who can propitiate God? Who has real knowledge of prayer, and with whom can that knowledge be shared? Are there any restrictions on religious experience because of gender, caste, birth, or heritage?

We have already seen that since Vedic times both men and women have been honored for their understanding and attainments of wisdom. So gender is not an issue which reflects upon aptitude. The questions of birth, nationality, or heritage have been vividly explained in the story of Satyakāma.

The Story of Satyakāma

Satyakāma grew up in a village near to Gautam Muni's aśrama. One day he went to the Muni and asked if he could study the Vedas. Gautam replied, "Who is your father, who is your mother, and by what authority do you wish to study the Vedas?"

Satyakāma replied, "I will ask my mother."

He went home to his mother and said, "Mother, I want to study the Vedas. Today I visited Gautam Muni's aśrama, and asked the Muni if he would teach me. He asked me, 'Who is your father, who is your mother, and by what authority do you wish to study the Vedas?' I told him that I would ask you. Mother, what answer should I give?"

His mother said, "Son, your father was a soldier in an army which camped outside our village. I only knew him for one night. My name is Jabali. Introduce yourself as Satyakāma, son of Jabali."

The next day Satyakāma returned to Gautam Muni's aśrama. He said to the Muni, "Sir, I would like to study the Vedas."

Gautam replied, "Who is your father, who is your mother, and by what authority do you wish to study the Vedas?"

"Sir," replied Satyakāma. "I asked that same question from my mother last night, and I will share with you the answer which she gave to me. She said, "Son, your father was a soldier in an army which camped outside our village. I only knew him for one night. My name is Jabali. Introduce yourself as Satyakāma, son of Jabali."

And all the other students began to shout, "Kick that impure boy outside the aśrama! He should not even be allowed inside! He doesn't even know his father's name! Get him out!"

Gautam Muni replied, "No. He is a brāhmaṇa. Only a brāhmaṇa can speak the truth without fear. Come Satyakāma, and sit by me. I will be pleased to be your Guru!"

Recitation of the Chaṇḍi Pāṭh

So how do we become the brāhmaṇas who have authority to perform sādhana, and what spiritual discipline should we perform? We would like to illustrate by our worship through the path of the Divine Mother, especially as it is described in the Chaṇḍi Pāṭh.

Although there are as many ways of reciting the Chaṇḍi Pāṭh as there are individuals, all the styles primarily break down into four categories: Bhakti Pāṭh, Śakti Pāṭh, Tapasyā, Jīvanam.

In a Bhakti Pāṭh read for meaning. Most of the Chaṇḍi Pāṭh is written in anuṣṭup chanda, 32 syllables to the verse. The Rule of Eights says that after every eight syllables there will be a pause.

Start with the Devyāḥ Kavacam, Athārgalā Stotram, Kīlakam, Navārṇa Vidhiḥ, and Siddha Kuñjikā Stotram.

In a Śakti Pāṭh, the most important ingredient is prāṇāyāma. Inhale your dikṣa mantra and pronounce 1, 2, or more verses per breath on the exhalation.

A pāṭh or recitation is performed for tapasyā when the most important focus is placed on āsana siddhi and prāṇāyāma, without changing the āsana until the saṅkalpa is complete.

An efficient way of attaining āsana siddhi in tapasyā is to perform homa, the recitation of mantras before the sacred fire.

The Chaṇḍi Yajna is the offering of oblations to the divine fire as specified in the system of worship. The Chaṇḍi Pāṭh from Chapters One through Thirteen consist of 700 ahutis. There 535 ślokas, 42 half ślokas, 57 uvācas, and 66 namastasyais, all total 700. The Chaṇḍi Pāṭh or Durgā Saptaśati does not really mean 700 Verses in praise of the Goddess, but rather 700 ahutis, or oblations.

It is customary that no offerings, no ahutis are made for the recitation of the Devyāḥ Kavacam, Athārgalā Stotram, and Kīlakam.

Pronunciation and the Chaṇḍi Samputs

In addition to sitting before the fire, there are other forms of tapasyā as well. Reciting the Chaṇḍi Pāṭh while sitting in cold water, in hot water, naked on snow, or surrounded by five fires (usually performed with fires in front, in back, and on the two sides, in the heat of summer with the sun overhead).

The process of Jīvanam means adding life to the mantra. In Jīvanam we invoke the nāda śakti by prolonging the life of the recitation. Every mantra has its origin in Oṁ and ends in Oṁ as well. We extend the sound coming from Oṁ while listening to the subtle sound within.

A Sīdhā Pāṭh, after the prefratory mantras and Saṅkalpa, begins with the Vedic Rātri Śuktam, includes the Navārṇa Vidhiḥ, encompasses the thirteen chapters, again the Navārṇa Vidhiḥ to the Vedic Devi Śuktam, Siddha Kuñjikā Stotram, and Praṇāmaḥ. The Śāpoddhāra mantras can also be added at the beginning and end.

The Ulaṭā Pāṭh, after the prefratory mantras and Saṅkalpa, begins with the Vedic Rātri Śuktam, includes the Navārṇa Vidhiḥ, and begins at the very end of Chapter thirteen with the words: Klīṁ Oṁ, and then recites each half śloka in reverse order. Therefore, the fifth chapter will say: Namastasyai Namo Namaḥ,Namastasyai, Namastasyai.

The Dhyānams are recited forwards as normal. At the end again the Navārṇa Vidhiḥ, the Vedic Devi Śuktam, Siddha Kuñjikā Stotram, and Praṇāmaḥ are performed.

There are other recitations which grant great fruits:
108 times Siddha Kuñjikā Stotram
108 times Durgā Dvātriṁśannāma Mālā
108 times Śrī Devyatharvaśīrṣam

A Samput Pāṭh is performed when the samput mantra is pronounced once before and once after each mantra qualifying for ahuti in the Chaṇḍi.

For example, Hrīṁ Sampuṭ will be pronounced before each mantra: Hrīṁ Oṁ Aiṁ Mārkeṇḍeya uvāca Hrīṁ
Hrīṁ Sāvarṇiḥ ...

Then the fifth chapter will sound like: Namastasyai Hrīṁ Hrīṁ, Namastasyai Hrīṁ Hrīṁ, Namastasyai Namo Namaḥ Hrīṁ Hrīṁ

The same will apply to the Navārṇa Sampuṭ, the Kādi Sampuṭ, or the Gāyatrī Sampuṭ.

It is important to only practice the samputṣ with the thirteen chapters. Just as no offerings, no ahutis, are made for the recitation of the Devyāḥ Kavacam, Athārgalā Stotram, and Kīlakam, in the same way no samputṣ are offered. The tradition says that putting on the armor, opening the bolt, and opening the pin are functions which prepare the worshipper to enter into the secret, and that the offerings should be made after having entered within.

The Udaya Samputṣ consist of different mantras for different purposes. Just as one would offer ahuti at the divine fire, in the same way the Samputṣ are offered.

There are many mantras which can be used. The following are some examples. References are made of chapter and verse from the Chaṇḍi Pāṭh.

1. For the welfare of the masses:

4 - 3

देव्या यया ततमिदं जगदात्मशक्त्या
निश्शेषदेवगणशक्तिसमूहमूर्त्या ।
तामम्बिकामखिलदेवमहर्षिपूज्यां
भक्त्या नताः स्म विदधातु शुभानि सा नः ॥

devyā yayā tatam idaṁ jagadāt maśaktyā
niśśeṣa devagaṇa śakti samūhamūrtyā |
tāmambikām akhila deva maharṣipūjyāṁ
bhaktyā natāḥ sma vidadhātu śubhāni sā naḥ ||

Her intrinsic nature is the aggregate energy of all the Gods; with Her energy She pervades the entire universe. She is the most highly regarded by all the Gods and Seers of sacred Wisdom. To the Mother of the Universe, with the greatest intensity of devotion, we give reverence unto Her. May She grant us all welfare.

2. To destroy impurity and fear from the universe:

4 - 4

यस्याः प्रभावमतुलं भगवाननन्तो
ब्रह्मा हरश्च न हि वक्तुमलं बलं च ।
सा चण्डिकाखिलजगत्परिपालनाय
नाशाय चाशुभभयस्य मतिं करोतु ॥

yasyāḥ prabhāvam atulaṁ bhagavān ananto
brahmā haraśca na hi vaktumalaṁ balaṁ ca |
sā caṇḍikākhila jagat pari pālanāya
nāśāya cāśubha bhayasya matiṁ karotu ||

Whose incomparable greatness and strength the Lord of the Universe (masculine) who creates, preserves, and dissolves the creation is incapable to extol, may that Supreme Empress, She Who Tears Apart Thought, think to protect the entire gross world and destroy fear and impurity.

3. To protect the universe:

4 - 5

या श्रीः स्वयं सुकृतिनां भवनेष्वलक्ष्मीः
पापात्मनां कृतधियां हृदयेषु बुद्धिः ।
श्रद्धा सतां कुलजनप्रभवस्य लज्जा
तां त्वां नताः स्म परिपालय देवि विश्वम् ॥

yā śrīḥ svayaṁ sukṛtināṁ bhavaneṣvalakṣmīḥ
pāpātmanāṁ kṛtadhiyāṁ hṛdayeṣu buddhiḥ |
śraddhā satāṁ kulajana prabhavasya lajjā
tāṁ tvāṁ natāḥ sma paripālaya devi viśvam ||

She is the Goddess of True Wealth in the homes of virtuous souls and is the misery of those who perform evil. She is Intelligence in the hearts of the pure minded, Faith to the truthful, and Humility to the truly noble. To that Divine Goddess we bow in reverence. Please protect the entire universe.

4. For the prosperity of the universe:

11 - 33

विश्वेश्वरि त्वं परिपासि विश्वं
विश्वात्मिका धारयसीति विश्वम् ।
विश्वेशवन्द्या भवती भवन्ति
विश्वाश्रया ये त्वयि भक्तिनम्राः ॥

viśveśvari tvaṁ paripāsi viśvaṁ
viśvātmikā dhārayasīti viśvam |
viśveśavandyā bhavatī bhavanti
viśvāśrayā ye tvayi bhakti namrāḥ ||

You are the Sovereign of the universe. You protect the universe. The soul of the universe, you support the universe. Those who bow to you with devotion become the refuge of the universe.

5. To destroy the difficulties of the inhabitants of the universe:

11 - 3

देवि प्रपन्नार्तिहरे प्रसीद

प्रसीद मातर्जगतोऽखिलस्य ।

प्रसीद विश्वेश्वरि पाहि विश्वं

त्वमीश्वरी देवि चराचरस्य ॥

devi prapannārti hare prasīda
prasīda mātar jagato-khilasya |
prasīda viśveśvari pāhi viśvaṁ
tvamīśvarī devi carācarasya ||

Oh Goddess, you who remove the distress of all who take refuge in you, be pleased. Be pleased, Oh Mother of the entire Perceivable World. Be pleased, Oh Supreme of the Universe; protect the universe. Oh Goddess, you are Supreme over all that moves and does not move.

6. For the remission of the sins of the universe:

\- 34 -

देवि प्रसीद परिपालय नोऽरिभीते

र्नित्यं यथासुरवधादधुनैव सद्यः ।

पापानि सर्वजगतां प्रशमं नयाशु

उत्पातपाकजनितांश्च महोपसर्गान् ॥

devi prasīda paripālaya no-ribhiter
nityaṁ yathāsura vadhādadhunaiva sadyaḥ |
pāpāni sarva jagatāṁ praśamaṁ nayāśu
utpātapāka janitāṁśca mahopasargān ||

Oh Goddess, please be pleased. As you have just now saved us by slaying thoughts, in like manner always save us from fear of foes.

Eradicate all evil from all the worlds, as well as all confusion and disturbance.

7. To destroy all difficulties:

11 - 12

शरणागतदीनार्तपरित्राणपरायणे ।

सर्वस्यार्त्तिहरे देवि नारायणि नमोऽस्तु ते ॥

śaraṇāgata dīnārta paritrāṇa parāyaṇe |
sarvasyārtti hare devi nārāyaṇi namo-stu te ||

Those who are devoted to you and take refuge in you, even though lowly and humble, you save them from all discomfort and unhappiness. All worry you take away, Oh Goddess, Exposer of Consciousness, we bow to you.

8. To destroy all difficulties and to replace with benificent circumstances:

5 - 81

स्तुता सुरैः पूर्वमभीष्टसंश्रयात्

तथा सुरेन्द्रेण दिनेषु सेविता ।

करोतु सा नः शुभहेतुरीश्वरी

शुभानि भद्राण्यभिहन्तु चापदः ॥

stutā suraiḥ pūrvamabhīṣṭa saṁśrayāt
tathā surendreṇa dineṣu sevitā |
karotu sā naḥ śubha hetur īśvarī
śubhāni bhadrāṇyabhi hantu cāpadaḥ ||

In days of old, all of the Gods, led by Indra, the Rule of the Pure, sang these verses of praise for the purpose of accomplishing their desired objective of surrendering the ego in the Light of Wisdom, and for many days that service was rendered. May She, the Seer of All, the Lord of All, the Source of All Good, perform similarly for us all auspicious things by putting an end to all distress.

9. To destroy all fear:

A. 11 - 24

सर्वस्वरूपे सर्वेशे सर्वशक्तिसमन्विते ।

भयेभ्यस्त्राहि नो देवि दुर्गे देवि नमोऽस्तु ते ॥

sarva svarūpe sarveśe sarva śakti samanvite I
bhayebhyastrāhi no devi durge devi namo-stu te II

The Intrinsic Nature of All, the Supreme of All, and the Energy of All as well; you remove all fear from us, Oh Goddess; Reliever of Difficulties, Oh Goddess, we bow to you.

B. 11 - 25

एतत्ते वदनं सौम्यं लोचनत्रयभूषितम् ।

पातु नः सर्वभीतिभ्यः कात्यायनि नमोऽस्तु ते ॥

etatte vadanaṁ saumyaṁ locana trayabhūṣitam I
pātu naḥ sarvabhītibhyaḥ kātyāyani namo-stu te II

May this beautiful face, displaying three eyes, protect us from all existence. Ever Pure One, we bow to you.

C. 11 - 26

ज्वालाकरालमत्युग्रमशेषासुरसूदनम् ।

त्रिशूलं पातु नो भीतेर्भद्रकालि नमोऽस्तु ते ॥

jvālākarālamatyugram aśeṣāsura sūdanam I
triśūlaṁ pātu no bhīter bhadrakāli namo-stu te II

With intensive brilliance, exceedingly sharp, the fierce destroyer of all thoughts, may your trident protect us from all fear. Oh Excellent She Who is Beyond All Time, we bow to you.

10. To destroy sin:

11 - 27

हिनस्ति दैत्यतेजांसि स्वनेनापूर्य या जगत् ।

सा घण्टा पातु नो देवि पापेभ्योऽनः सुतानिव ॥

hinasti daitya tejāṁsi svanenāpūrya yā jagat |
sā ghaṇṭā pātu no devi pāpebhyo-naḥ sutāniva ||

Oh Goddess, the loud sound of your bell fills the perceivable world, destroying the prowess of all thoughts, and protecting us from evil as a Mother protects Her children.

11. To destroy illness:

11 - 29

रोगानशेषानपहंसि तुष्टा

रुष्टा तु कामान् सकलानभीष्टान् ।

त्वामाश्रितानां न विपन्नराणां

त्वमाश्रिता ह्याश्रयतां प्रयान्ति ॥

rogānaśeṣā napahaṁsi tuṣṭā
ruṣṭā tu kāmān sakalān abhīṣṭān |
tvāmāśritānāṁ na vipannarāṇāṁ
tvamāśritā hyāśrayatāṁ prayānti ||

When you are pleased, you destroy all infirmities, and when you are displeased, you frustrate all desires. No calamity befalls those who take refuge in you, and those who take refuge in you invariably become a refuge to others.

12. To destroy the great death:

athārgalā stotram - 1

ॐ जयन्ती मङ्गला काली भद्रकाली कपालिनी ।

दुर्गा क्षमा शिवा धात्री स्वाहा स्वधा नमोऽस्तु ते ॥

oṁ jayantī maṅgalā kālī bhadra-kālī kapālinī |
durgā kṣamā śivā dhātrī svāhā svadhā namo-stu te ||
Oṁ She Who Conquers Over All, All-Auspicious, the Remover of Darkness, the Excellent One Beyond Time, the Bearer of the Skulls of Impure Thought, the Reliever of Difficulties, Loving Forgiveness, Supporter of the Universe, Oblations of I am One with God, Oblations of Ancestral Praise, to You, we bow.

13. To become free from disease and to attain good fortune:

athārgalā stotram - 12 -

देहि सौभाग्यमारोग्यं देहि मे परमं सुखम् ।

रूपं देहि जयं देहि यशो देहि द्विषो जहि ॥

dehi saubhāgyamārogyaṁ
dehi me paramaṁ sukham |
rūpaṁ dehi jayaṁ dehi yaśo dehi dviṣo jahi ||
Give beauty, freedom from disease; give me supreme happiness. Give us your form, give us victory, give us welfare, remove all hostility.

14. To get an excellent spouse:

athārgalā stotram - 24

पत्नीं मनोरमां देहि मनोवृत्तानुसारिणीम् ।

तारिणीं दुर्गसंसार सागरस्य कुलोद्भवाम् ॥

patnīṁ manoramāṁ dehi manovṛttānusāriṇīm |
tāriṇīṁ durga saṁsāra sāgarasya kulodbhavām ||
Give me a wife in harmony with my mind, who follows the changes of mind, and who can lead a family of noble birth across the difficulties of the ocean of objects and their relationships.

15. To remove all obstacles:

11 - 39

सर्वाबाधाप्रशमनं त्रैलोक्यस्याखिलेश्वरि ।

एवमेव त्वया कार्यमस्मद्वैरिविनाशनम् ॥

sarvā bādhā praśamanaṁ trailokyasyākhileśvari |
evameva tvayā kāryam asmad vairivināśanam ||

Oh Spirit of the Supreme Sovereign, terminate all disturbance in the three worlds, and in like manner, remove from us all hostility.

16. To give birth to excellent fate and welfare:

4 - 15

ते सम्मता जनपदेषु धनानि तेषां

तेषां यशांसि न च सीदति धर्मवर्गः ।

धन्यास्त एव निभृतात्मजभृत्यदारा

येषां सदाभ्युदयदा भवती प्रसन्ना ॥

te sammatā janapadeṣu dhanāni teṣāṁ
teṣāṁ yaśāṁsi na ca sīdati dharma vargaḥ |
dhanyāsta eva nibhṛtāt majabhṛtyadārā
yeṣaṁ sadābhyudayadā bhavatī prasannā ||

Oh you who are the Grantor of all Welfare, those with whom you are pleased are certainly respected in their country. They are endowed with welfare, and their acts of Wisdom and Harmony do not perish. They are blessed by the devotion of their children, wives, and servants.

17. To destroy the pain of affliction:

4 - 17

दुर्गे स्मृता हरसि भीतिमशेषजन्तोः

स्वस्थैः स्मृता मतिमतीव शुभां ददासि ।

दारिद्र्यदुःखभयहारिणि का त्वदन्या

सर्वोपकारकरणाय सदाऽऽर्द्रचित्ता ॥

durge smṛtā harasi bhītima śeṣa jantoḥ
svasthaiḥ smṛtā matimatīva śubhāṁ dadāsi |
dāridrya duḥkha bhayahāriṇi kā tvadanyā
sarvopakāra karaṇāya sadā--rdracittā ||

Oh Reliever of Difficulties, remembering you the fear of all living beings is dispelled. When remembered by those individuals in the harmony of spiritual growth, you increase their welfare and intelligence. Who is like you, Oh Dispeller of Poverty, Pain, and Fear, whose sympathetic demeanor always extends compassionate assistance to everyone?

18. To acquire protection:

4 - 24 -

शूलेन पाहि नो देवि पाहि खड्गेन चाम्बिके ।

घण्टास्वनेन नः पाहि चापज्यानिःस्वनेन च ॥

śūlena pāhi no devi pāhi khaḍgena cāmbike |
ghaṇṭā svanena naḥ pāhi cāpajyāniḥ svanena ca ||

Oh Goddess, protect us with your spear; Mother of the Universe, protect us with your sword. Protect us with the sound of your bell, and protect us with the twang of your bow string.

19. To achieve all knowledge and to perceive all women as Divine Mother:

11 - 6

विद्याः समस्तास्तव देवि भेदाः
स्त्रियः समस्ताः सकला जगत्सु ।
त्वयैकया पूरितमम्बयैतत्
का ते स्तुतिः स्तव्यपरा परोक्तिः ॥

vidyāḥ samastāstava devi bhedāḥ
striyaḥ samastāḥ sakalā jagatsu |
tvayaikayā pūritamambayaitat
kā te stutiḥ stavyaparā paroktiḥ ||

Oh Goddess, all that is knowable are your various distinctions, and all women in the world reflect your capacity entirely. By you, Oh Mother, this world is filled. For you who are beyond praise, how can we sing of your glory?

20. To attain all manner of welfare:

11 - 10

सर्वमङ्गलमङ्गल्ये शिवे सर्वार्थसाधिके ।
शरण्ये त्र्यम्बके गौरि नारायणि नमोऽस्तु ते ॥

sarva maṅgala maṅgalye śive sarvārtha sādhike |
śaraṇye tryambake gauri nārāyaṇi namo-stu te ||

To the Auspicious of all Auspiciousness, to the Good, to the Accomplisher of all Objectives, to the Source of Refuge, to the Mother of the Three Worlds, to the Goddess Who is Rays of Light, Exposer of Consciousness, we bow to you.

21. To acquire greater energy:

11 - 11

सृष्टिस्थितिविनाशानां शक्तिभूते सनातनि ।

गुणाश्रये गुणमये नारायणि नमोऽस्तु ते ॥

sṛṣṭi sthiti vināśānāṁ śakti bhūte sanātani |
guṇāśraye guṇamaye nārāyaṇi namo-stu te ||

You are the Eternal Energy of Creation, Preservation, and Destruction in all existence; that upon which all qualities depend, that which limits all qualities, Exposer of Consciousness, we bow to you.

22. To achieve satisfaction:

11 - 35

प्रणतानां प्रसीद त्वं देवि विश्वार्तिहारिणि ।

त्रैलोक्यवासिनामीड्ये लोकानां वरदा भव ॥

praṇatānāṁ prasīda tvaṁ devi viśvārtihāriṇi |
trailokya vāsinā mīḍye lokānāṁ varadā bhava ||

Oh Goddess, Remover of the sufferings and calamities of the universe, be gracious to us who bow down to you. You who are worthy of praise by the inhabitants of the three worlds, grant the best to all the worlds.

23. To be saved from various problems:

11 - 32

रक्षांसि यत्रोग्रविषाश्च नागा

यत्रारयो दस्युबलानि यत्र ।

दावानलो यत्र तथाब्धिमध्ये

तत्र स्थिता त्वं परिपासि विश्वम् ॥

rakṣāṁsi yatro graviṣāśca nāgā
yatrārayo dasyubalāni yatra |
dāvānalo yatra tathābdhimadhye
tatra sthitā tvaṁ paripāsi viśvam ||

Where there are demons of confused thoughts, serpents of dreadful poison, where there are foes and mighty hosts of robbers, where there is a great conflagration, in the midst of the sea of objects and their relationships, you stand and save the universe.

24. To be free from obstacles and be blessed with wealth and children:

11 - 39

सर्वाबाधाप्रशमनं त्रैलोक्यस्याखिलेश्वरि ।

एवमेव त्वया कार्यमस्मद्वैरिविनाशनम् ॥

sarvā bādhā praśamanaṁ trailokyasyākhileśvari |
evameva tvayā kāryam asmad vairivināśanam ||

Oh Spirit of the Supreme Sovereign, terminate all disturbance in the three worlds, and in like manner, remove from us all hostility.

25. To achieve enjoyment and liberation:

athārgalā stotram - 14

विधेहि देवि कल्याणं विधेहि परमां श्रियम् ।

रूपं देहि जयं देहि यशो देहि द्विषो जहि ॥

vidhehi devi kalyāṇaṁ vidhehi paramāṁ śriyam |
rūpaṁ dehi jayaṁ dehi yaśo dehi dviṣo jahi ||

Oh Goddess, grant welfare, grant supreme prosperity. Give us your form, give us victory, give us welfare, remove all hostility.

26. To destroy sin and acquire devotion:

athārgalā stotram - 9

नतेभ्यः सर्वदा भक्त्या चण्डिके दुरितापहे ।

रूपं देहि जयं देहि यशो देहि द्विषो जहि ॥

natebhyaḥ sarvadā bhaktyā caṇḍike duritāpahe |
rūpaṁ dehi jayaṁ dehi yaśo dehi dviṣo jahi ||

For those who bow to you with devotion, you remove all distress. Give us your form, give us victory, give us welfare, remove all hostility.

27. To attain heaven and liberation:

11 - 7

सर्वभूता यदा देवी स्वर्गमुक्तिप्रदायिनी ।

त्वं स्तुता स्तुतये का वा भवन्तु परमोक्तयः ॥

sarva bhūtā yadā devī svarga mukti pradāyinī |
tvaṁ stutā stutaye kā vā bhavantu paramoktayaḥ ||

Oh Goddess, Bestower of Heaven and Liberation, you are all existence. When you have been thus extolled, what else can be sung of your glory?

28. To attain heaven and liberation:

11 - 8

सर्वस्य बुद्धिरूपेण जनस्य हृदि संस्थिते ।

स्वर्गापवर्गदे देवि नारायणि नमोऽस्तु ते ॥

sarvasya buddhirūpeṇa janasya hṛdi saṁsthite |
svargā pavargade devi nārāyaṇi namo-stu te ||

You reside in the hearts of all living beings in the form of Intelligence. You bestow upon your devotees heaven and liberation. Oh Goddess, Exposer of Consciousness, we bow to you.

29. To attain liberation:

11 - 5

त्वं वैष्णवी शक्तिरनन्तवीर्या
विश्वस्य बीजं परमासि माया ।
सम्मोहितं देवि समस्तमेतत्
त्वं वै प्रसन्ना भुवि मुक्तिहेतुः ॥

tvaṁ vaiṣṇavī śaktir anantavīryā
viśvasya bījaṁ paramāsi māyā |
sammohitaṁ devi samastametat
tvaṁ vai prasannā bhuvi mukti hetuḥ ||

You are the Energy of The Consciousness That Pervades All, of infinite valor, the Seed of the Universe, that which is beyond limitation. By you, Oh Goddess, all is deluded by attachment, and if you are gracious, you are the cause of liberation in this world.

30. To know whether a dream is true or untrue:

दुर्गे देवि नमस्तुभ्यं सर्वकामार्थसाधिके ।
मम सिद्धिमसिद्धिं वा स्वप्ने सर्वं प्रदर्शय ॥

durge devi namastubhyaṁ sarvakāmārthasādhike |
mama siddhimasiddhiṁ vā svapne sarvaṁ pradarśaya ||

Oh Goddess Durga, we bow down to you, Giver of the objects of all desires to sādhus. Show me all of my attainments and failures in my dreams.

In an Asta Samput there are five mantras for each verse, pronounced: Sīdhā - Ulaṭa - Saptaśati - Ulaṭa - Sīdhā.

शरणागतदीनार्तपरित्राणपरायणे ।
सर्वस्यार्त्तिहरे देवि नारायणि नमोऽस्तु ते ॥

सर्वस्यार्त्तिहरे देवि नारायणि नमोऽस्तु ते ॥

शरणागतदीनार्तपरित्राणपरायणे ।

Saptaśati mantra

सर्वस्यार्त्तिहरे देवि नारायणि नमोऽस्तु ते ॥

शरणागतदीनार्तपरित्राणपरायणे ।

शरणागतदीनार्तपरित्राणपरायणे ।

सर्वस्यार्त्तिहरे देवि नारायणि नमोऽस्तु ते ॥

Śatākṣara viddhiḥ:

ॐ जातवेदसे सुनवाम सोमम-रातीयतोनि दहाति वेदः ।

स नः पर्षदति दुर्गाणि विश्वा नावेव सिन्धुं दुरितात्यग्निः ॥

oṁ jātavedase sunavāma somam
arātīyatoni dahāti vedaḥ
sa naḥ parṣadati durgāṇi viśvā
nāveva sindhuṁ duritātyagniḥ

Oṁ We worship the Knower of All with the offering of Love and Devotion. May the God of Purity reduce all enmity in the universe to ashes, and as an excellent oarsman, may he steer our ship across the sea of pain and confusion to the shores of Liberation.

ॐ भूर्भुवः स्वः

तत् सवितुर्वरेण्यम् भर्गो देवस्य धीमहि ।

धियो यो नः प्रचोदयात् ॥

oṁ bhūr bhuvaḥ svaḥ
tat savituÑvareṇyam bhargo devasya dhīmahi
dhiyo yo naḥ pracodayāt

Oṁ the Infinite Beyond Conception, the gross body, the subtle body and the causal body; we meditate upon that Light of Wisdom which is the Supreme Wealth of the Gods. May it grant to us increase in our meditations.

त्र्यम्बकं यजामहे सुगन्धिं पुष्टिवर्द्धनम् ।
उर्व्वारुकमिव बन्धनान्मृत्योर्म्मुक्षीयमामृतात् ॥

tryambakaṁ yajāmahe
sugandhiṁ puṣṭivarddhanam
urvvārukamiva bandhanānmṛtyormmukṣīyamāmṛtāt

We adore the Father of the three worlds, of excellent fame, Grantor of Increase. As a cucumber is released from its bondage to the stem, so may we be freed from Death to dwell in immortality.

The one hundred lettered sampuṭ actually consists of one hundred five letters. There are 44 syllables in the Triṣṭup Chandaḥ mantra, 24 in the Gāyatrī, 32 in the Anuṣṭup, equals 100 syllables, plus the five syllables in the Gāyatrī Vyahriti,

ॐ भूर्भुवः स्वः

oṁ bhūr bhuvaḥ svaḥ

This description of some of the advanced sādhanas that relate to the Chaṇḍi Pāṭh are by no means intended to suggest that seekers should try them on their own. Obviously you should seek advice and direction from your Guru as you proceed. My attempt here is to preserve some of the teachings from the oral traditions in a written form, and to empower seekers of the future with greater understanding.

If you could just be in the same vicinity where such sādhanas are being performed, you would have a greater idea of the intensity of vibrations that flow from the continuous recitation of the Chaṇḍi Pāṭh according to the rules of prāṇāyāma. Then attention becomes submerged into the vibrations of the Goddess, we leave the apprehension of our bodies, and become witness to the meaning of the Chaṇḍi. Rather then spending our time with critique of the accents or pronunciation of others, we appreciate every effort that sincere seekers make in the furtherance of their spiritual objectives, while at the same time we pursue our own.

More Books by Shree Maa and Swami Satyananda Saraswati

Annapūrṇa Thousand Names
Before Becoming This
Bhagavad Gītā
Chaṇḍi Pāṭh
Chaṇḍi Pāṭh - Study of Chapter One
Chaṇḍi Pāṭh - Study of Chapter Two
Cosmic Pūjā
Cosmic Pūjā Bengali
Devī Gītā
Devī Mandir Songbook
Durgā Pūjā Beginner
Ganeśa Pūjā
Gāyatrī Sahasra Nāma
Guru Gītā
Hanumān Pūjā
Kālī Pūjā
Lakṣmī Sahasra Nāma
Lalitā Triśati
Pronunciation and the Chaṇḍi Samputs
Rudrāṣṭādhyāyī
Sahib Sadhu
Saraswati Pūjā for Children
Shree Maa's Favorite Recipes
Shree Maa - The Guru & the Goddess
Shree Maa, The Life of a Saint
Śiva Pūjā Beginner
Śiva Pūjā and Advanced Fire Ceremony
Sundara Kāṇḍa
Swāmī Purāṇa
Thousand Names of Gāyatrī
Thousand Names of Viṣṇu and
Satya Nārāyaṇa Vrata Kathā

Pronunciation and the Chaṇḍi Sampuṭs

CDs and Cassettes

Chaṇḍi Pāṭh
Durgā Pūjā Beginner
Lalitā Triśati
Mantras of the Nine Planets
Navarṇa Mantra
Oh Dark Night Mother
Oṁ Mantra
Sādhu Stories from the Himalayas
Shree Maa at the Devi Mandir
Shree Maa in the Temple of the Heart
Shiva is in My Heart
Shree Maa on Tour, 1998
Śiva Pūjā Beginner
Śiva Pūjā and Advanced Fire Ceremony
The Goddess is Everywhere
The Songs of Ramprasad
The Thousand Names of Kālī
Tryambakaṁ Mantra

Videos

Across the States with Shree Maa & Swamiji
Meaning and Method of Worship
Shree Maa: Meeting a Modern Saint
Visiting India with Shree Maa and Swamiji

Please visit us at www.shreemaa.org
Our email is info@shreemaa.org

Lightning Source UK Ltd.
Milton Keynes UK
UKHW011335280622
405074UK00001B/90

9 781877 795107